The Islands of Bermuda

Another World

David F. Raine

MACMILLAN

First published 1990
Reprinted 1994

Published by THE MACMILLAN PRESS LTD
London and Basingstoke
Associated companies and representatives in Accra,
Auckland, Delhi, Dublin, Gaborone, Hamburg, Harare,
Hong Kong, Kuala Lumpur, Lagos, Manzini, Melbourne,
Mexico City, Nairobi, New York, Singapore, Tokyo

ISBN 0–333–51623–0

Printed in Hong Kong

A CIP catalogue record for this book is available from
the British Library.

Contents

For
PAMELA,
forever
my source of encouragement
and support

Acknowledgements
Cover picture: Jill Amos Raine

Other books by David Raine:
'The Pregnant Father'
'Sir George Somers — a man and his times'
'Pitseolak — a Canadian Tragedy'
'The Historic Towne of St George'
'Bermuda as it used to be'
'Architecture Bermuda style'

| Introduction |

Bermuda is somehow quite different from all of the other islands which grace this fair planet.

Perhaps the difference lies in the white-roofed cottages which pepper the green landscape with pastel shades of pink, yellow and blue. It may be the crystal clear waters which gently break along the shoreline. There is something unusual about Bermuda, an elegance here which can be seen in many different ways. It shows itself in rows of tall, slender palm trees and in carefully trimmed hedges of hibiscus in bloom; it can be seen in the graceful flight of a longtail circling for fish near the reefs. Then there is the pride and courtesy of the people themselves, for Bermudians are justifiably famous for their friendliness and their sense of style — whether they are dressing for work, the beach, the garden or church.

There is elegance also in the white frontage of an eighteenth century mansion, partially hidden by lush tropical vegetation somewhere in the back streets of St George. Columns reach upwards to link into a decorative wooden balcony; black shutters project from its windows; a broad limestone chimney peeps from somewhere beyond the roof-line. Nearby, a child in school uniform carries books, skips along the narrow roadway and starts her day. This too shows a face of Bermuda's elegant heritage.

Local calypsonian Hubert Smith once wrote a song entitled: 'Bermuda is another world'. He may very well be right. There is indeed nowhere else quite like these elegant

Bermudian beach. (BERMUDA TOURISM)

islands which lie in the mid-Atlantic — at peace with themselves and in harmony with the rest of the world. It is hoped that this book will help the reader to appreciate why.

David F. Raine
St David's Island
Bermuda

July 1988

Gibb's Hill Lighthouse. DAVID F. RAINE

| 1 |
Such remarkable origins...

Surveying the tranquil and undulating scenery from atop **Gibb's Hill Lighthouse**, it is almost impossible to imagine that such a serene landscape could be the result of a fiery volcanic eruption. But it is. Seismologists speculate that roughly a hundred million years ago a crack formed in the earth's crust in this part of the Atlantic and molten lava suddenly burst through, ripping the ocean's floor with such violence that rocks and ash were blasted from the watery depths and high into the sky above the water. The heat was so intense that the water itself must have bubbled and boiled for many months, possibly even for years.

When the unseen eruption subsided, the tip of the volcano was barely discernible above the water-line but it was that small speck of land upon which Bermuda would eventually grow. Carried from the Caribbean by the Gulf Stream, millions of microscopic coral polyps fastened themselves to the steep sides of the outcrop, growing one upon the other until an extensive reef had smothered the eroding core of the original volcano. In turn, over thousands of years, waves broke the dainty coral formations into a fine sand which was washed ashore and blown into hilly dunes. These eventually hardened and became the foundation of Bermuda's modern landscape. It is still hard to visualise that the gentle rolling countryside which we see today is really a sequence of fossilised sand-dunes solidly perched atop the long-extinct cap of a volcano.

We can safely assume that a succession of seeds and plants from the south drifted ashore and gradually established Bermuda's natural vegetation. Birds, unquestionably forced into landing here by inclement weather conditions during their flights over this part of the Atlantic, began to linger and build their nests among the rocks and crags; fish appeared along the reefs which loop the islands, finding refuge from the larger predators which prowl the deeper waters of the adjacent ocean.

Remarkable as it may seem, Bermuda remained entirely uninhabited until the seventeenth century. There is, however, some factual evidence to argue the case that these islands were actually the idyllic lands which were spoken of in Greek mythology; that they may have been the root of the Atlantis legend and that St Brendan himself may have drifted here in his endless quest for a natural Utopia. They were certainly the inspiration which William Shakespeare found for his play *The Tempest*.

These uninhabited islands were apparently first sighted in the year 1505 by the legendary Spanish explorer, Juan de Bermudez. However, he seems to have made no attempt to land here. Rather, he opted to sail cautiously along the outer reef so that his cartographer could take notes and draw some outlines, before continuing back to Europe. The direct result was the appearance of 'Las Bermudas' for the first time on a map. They are clearly identified on Peter Martyr's publication of 1511.

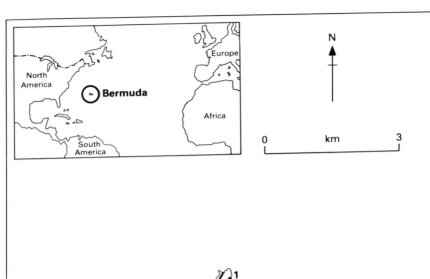

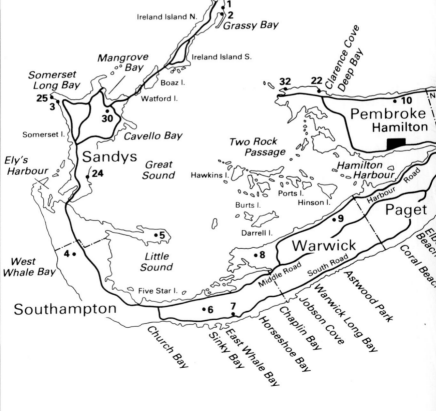

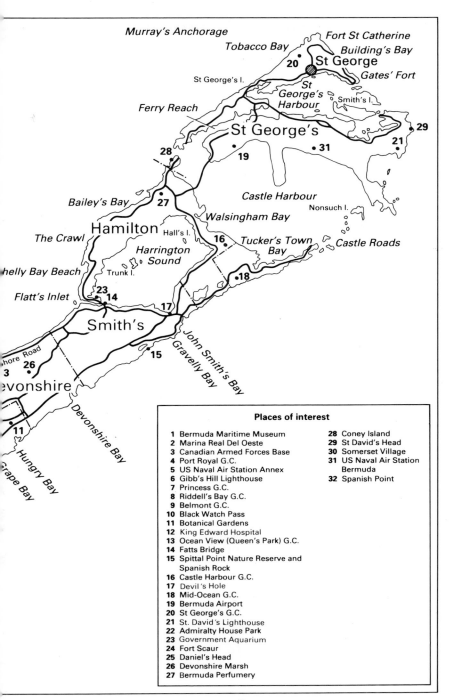

Places of interest

1 Bermuda Maritime Museum
2 Marina Real Del Oeste
3 Canadian Armed Forces Base
4 Port Royal G.C.
5 US Naval Air Station Annex
6 Gibb's Hill Lighthouse
7 Princess G.C.
8 Riddell's Bay G.C.
9 Belmont G.C.
10 Black Watch Pass
11 Botanical Gardens
12 King Edward Hospital
13 Ocean View (Queen's Park) G.C.
14 Fatts Bridge
15 Spittal Point Nature Reserve and Spanish Rock
16 Castle Harbour G.C.
17 Devil's Hole
18 Mid-Ocean G.C.
19 Bermuda Airport
20 St George's G.C.
21 St. David's Lighthouse
22 Admiralty House Park
23 Government Aquarium
24 Fort Scaur
25 Daniel's Head
26 Devonshire Marsh
27 Bermuda Perfumery
28 Coney Island
29 St David's Head
30 Somerset Village
31 US Naval Air Station Bermuda
32 Spanish Point

3

Nevertheless, although their precise location was obviously known to mariners, there is no evidence to show that anyone managed to set foot here for a further two decades. This is somewhat surprising, because both the Spanish and the Portuguese were sending out vessels into and beyond these waters at a rate averaging twenty per year during this period. Undeniably, there had emerged a consensus of opinion that Bermuda could not be expected to yield any gold bullion — which was unashamedly the prime motive for their venturing further southwards into Mexico and South America. There was also some justifiable fear of the uncharted reefs, which had regularly been claiming the vessels of those who were carried too close to shore. Finally, there was the rapidly growing myth that these were 'The Islands of Devils' — a notion fuelled by the hideous screeching sounds which had reportedly been heard often by ships sailing past in the night. (These sounds would later be identified as the call of nesting cahows!)

In 1515, Gonzalo Fernandez de Oviedo y Valdez entered in his log an unsuccessful bid to land a small party of men on Bermuda, but inclement weather and harsh seas thwarted the attempt. The effort, however, did enjoy some success in that it enabled the good Captain to be sufficiently close to produce the first detailed records of what this isolated and enigmatic group of islands was truly like. Ten years later, in 1525, the Portuguese Captain Estevan Gomez successfully anchored his flagship several times at different locations off the reefs and thereby managed to produce the first detailed map of 'Las Bermudas'. But still neither he nor his men ever claimed to have set foot on dry land.

The first human footprints ever known to have appeared on any of Bermuda's pink

Right ***The Tall Ship*** (*Simon Bolivar*). ***An example of the kind of vessel the first settlers arrived in.*** (DAVID F. RAINE)
Below: ***A South Shore beach.*** (DAVID F. RAINE)

4

beaches were those of Captain Bartholomew Carreno, whose logbook records that he stayed here 'exploring' for one month, in 1538. Such unprecedented activity, however, was not the product of bravery; nor was it in pursuit of the romantic ideal of merely 'being the first . . .' . As it so happened, the intrepid Captain Carreno and his followers were acting under the direct orders of the King of Spain himself. Charles V had issued explicit instructions that the crew must make a landing at all costs, in search of possible survivors from a Spanish fleet which had been lost two years earlier. Such concern from the noble monarch had nothing to do with humanity, however. Instead, the landing was motivated by rumours that his missing galleons had been heavily laden with gold and other priceless riches.

The second landing on record occurred in 1543. In that year, for reasons quite unknown to anyone, someone sat along the South Shore — at what is now appropriately known as 'Spanish Rock' — and carved the date. Well-founded speculation, based upon solid research, suggests that it was made by one of roughly thirty shipwrecked sailors from a Portuguese ship which foundered on the reef. We will probably never know his full identity.

Shipwrecks apparently occurred intermittently between that time and 1593, when a large French vessel under the charge of a very colourful pirate named Captain La Barbotière beached itself along the South Shore. On board was an equally interesting Englishman called Henry May. The seafaring Mr May's involvement with the swash-buckling Frenchmen was, at the very best, purely coincidental. He had originally left England in 1591, on an expedition into the South Pacific with James Lancaster, but on their way back through the Caribbean Lancaster was obliged to delay his return to England. With some urgency afoot, the hapless Henry May changed vessels at sea and hitched a ride to Europe with La Barbotière. The crew partied on wine, mistook their location and ground firmly on to Bermuda's coral. They stayed here for several months carrying out extensive repairs to the sadly battered hull. On the positive side, the outcome was a most intimate description of these islands, in English, which was received with much interest by the business community of London.

The continuous settlement of Bermuda did not occur until 1609 — once again the result of a shipwreck. In that year, whilst leading a convoy from England to the fledgling colony of Virginia, Sir George Somers had the misfortune to run foul of a violent storm which had brewed up in mid-Atlantic. Separated from the rest of his fleet and in imminent danger of sinking, the *Sea Venture* smashed into the eastern reefs off what is now **Fort St Catherine**. With all passengers and crew safely ashore, Somers and his party set about building themselves two new vessels, so that they could proceed on their intended route. Ten months later they slipped cautiously between heads of corals and sandy flatts, successfully turning towards Jamestown, in Virginia.

Somers left two men behind to establish sovereignty over the thoroughly explored islands; another remained with them when the Admiral returned in 1610. Almost incredibly, he had come back ostensibly to acquire more food for the hungry Virginians. Unfortunately, he became ill and died in Bermuda a short while later. In 1612, the first settlers arrived aboard the *Plough*. These extraordinary islands were finally to become inhabited.

| 2 |
The greatest tempest of them all!

The history of man's earliest attempts to cross the Atlantic Ocean is littered with tales about sudden storms, mountainous waves and wrecked ships. The diaries of those who made these early voyages are full of encounters with rough seas, swirling winds and angry clouds. More than a few, of course, also refer to seeing strange monsters and the phenomenon known as St Elmo's fire, an astonishing display of lights which fastened on to masts and illuminated entire vessels in a blinding glow, before suddenly disappearing once more into the darkness.

There is no doubt, however, that Bermudians regard the most significant of these dramas as the famous shipwreck which occurred in 1609, the one which directly resulted in the permanent settlement of Bermuda.

To appreciate fully the nature of this important event, it needs to be placed briefly in some sort of historical context. Throughout the sixteenth century, England had been increasingly dominating the high seas, gradually wresting both laurels and crowns from the heads of the oceanic pioneers of Spain and Portugal. By the late 1500s, England had already made some ill-fated attempts to colonise the vast continent of North America and with the dawn of the new century her efforts became even more determined. In 1607, a group of settlers was landed along the shores of the Chesapeake Bay where they built the settlement which became Jamestown.

Under the sponsorship of the Virginia Company, these willing English adventurers promptly set about the tasks of home-building, farming and hunting; however, their enthusiasm was not to be rewarded by proportional successes. By the end of the first year, many had died as a result of being ill-equipped to face the bitterly cold winter. Others had suffered from sickness or been killed during increasing hostilities with the neighbourhood Indians. Most had experienced extreme hunger. By 1608, their numbers had fallen dramatically from several hundred to a few dozen and a desperate report was sent back to England. It was made abundantly clear to the Company's shareholders in London that faith and goodwill were simply not adequate substitutes for the general ineptitude of many of the settlers. A gallant dandy from the fashionable streets of London was quite misplaced trying to track forest wildlife in a blizzard; an Essex farmhand was equally incompetent against a tomahawk wielded in hand-to-hand combat.

In 1609, determined not to lose this tender foothold on such a vast, unexplored territory, the Virginia Company dispatched a full fleet laden with fresh supplies of food, equipment, soldiers and more settlers. Sir George Somers was appointed Admiral of the fleet, entrusted with the responsibility of ensuring that they all reached

Statue of Sir George Somers, by Bermudian sculptor, Desmond Fountain.
(DAVID F. RAINE)

Jamestown safely. With him was Sir George Yeardley, Commander of the land forces responsible for the defence of the colony. Also in the party was Sir Thomas Gates, the new Lieutenant-Governor of Jamestown. On 15th May, seven ships sailed from the Woolwich dock in London; on 20th May, they grouped at the southern English port of Plymouth where they were joined by two other vessels, including *Sea Venture* with Somers standing squarely on the bridge, the lord surveying his bobbing domain.

8

Finally, on 2nd June, 1609, with all supplies and personnel firmly placed on board, this relief fleet of nine boats headed out into the Atlantic Ocean. The sun was setting, casting orange and pink hues along the cliffs and into the bays. For many of those huddled on the decks that evening, it was to be the last sunset they would ever see over land.

After seven weeks of relatively calm seas and light, favourable winds, the fleet was about one thousand miles west of the Azores when suddenly the weather changed. It was Monday, 24th July. Dark cumulo-nimbus clouds rolled in from beneath the horizon; tranquil waters suddenly erupted with grey fury. Waves blasted the boats helplessly from side to side and coupled with violent winds to rip the fleet apart. From the stern of *Sea Venture*, Somers spied the small pinnace *Catch* being battered by a vicious rogue wave; they threw a safety rope to the helpless and beleaguered ship in hopes of saving her, but were soon forced to cut it free out of fear that the two boats might collide and sink. Captain Philes and his valiant crew were never seen again; in England, there would be more widows, more orphans.

The storm raged throughout the night without abating. Captains bellowed unheard commands into the darkness; crewmen pulled ropes, slipped, and struggled to move on. Beyond view, the wind whipped the pointed crests of the waves into a tattered foam which it then hurled at the creaking hulls and ripped sails. Late on Tuesday, the Captain of the *Sea Venture*, Christopher Newport, went below deck and confirmed his worst fears — the planking of his boat had sprung a serious leak beneath the water-line; the ship was in imminent danger of sinking. They now could neither hear nor see any others from the fleet; they were quite alone with the violence of the Atlantic.

For a full three days those on board the *Sea Venture* fought to keep alive. Without relief, the men stood knee-deep in water bailing ceaselessly to remain afloat, whilst unforgiving waves relentlessly pounded their ship from the outside. Gale-force winds splintered the masts and whistled through the ragged canvasses. Somers, Gates, Yeardley and Newport all took their places in the swampy darkness below decks and exhausted womenfolk tended to the needs of the injured and the hungry. The Reverend Richard Bucke suffered and prayed alongside the rest, urging them to have faith whilst he bailed; calling, perhaps pleading, for some fairly rapid and inspired Divine intervention.

By Thursday, they were all close to total exhaustion. The relentless storm, however, was very much alive and the *Sea Venture* was facing the real possibility that it might suddenly be caught off-balance and keel over. As a further safeguard Captain Newport ordered that all superfluous luggage and equipment should be tossed overboard; things had become desperate. Even the hardiest of his crew had begun to realise the hopelessness of their dilemma; without a miracle, they were sure to perish before another day had passed. For just a moment they managed to ignore the fury of the elements outside and an atmosphere of solemnity slowly descended over the ship. They stood alone or huddled in small groups to accept their fate. Some even broke open a cask of wine and offered a final toast to one another.

Overleaf: *Visitors at Fort St Catherine, today.* (BERMUDA TOURISM)

Finally, on Friday, 28th July, 1609, land was sighted. Sir George Somers knew full well that this would have to be the legendary 'Bermudas', for he had sailed past them once before and their location had been long since plotted on the maps of the time. But surely Providence had dropped them there that day, when the *Sea Venture* was so ominously close to sinking beneath the waves. The Reverend Bucke cheerfully led the bedraggled assembly in offering the most heartfelt of thanks to the merciful Almighty.

Without loss of life, Captain Newport wedged his vessel between some reefs off the eastern end of Bermuda and everyone gratefully made a safe landfall on St George's Island near to where Fort St Catherine now stands. As the ship gently nudged herself deeper and deeper into the fragile coral reef, the relieved crew and passengers ferried whatever could be salvaged on to the crescent-shaped beach which lay close to where the ship was so precariously balanced. A few days later, from the safety of the sands, they watched as she slipped gently from her perch and gradually glided out of sight, deep down into the clear waters which would be her tomb.

The remarkable maiden voyage of the *Sea Venture* had come to a close. Never again would the beautiful 'Islands of Devils' be uninhabited. In distant London, the shipwreck inspired William Shakespeare to write his celebrated play *The Tempest*.

| 3 |
System of government

The islands of Bermuda are located at 64°W and 32°N, and cover approximately twenty-one square miles in the vastness of the North Atlantic Ocean. According to the figures released in 1985, the population was 57 000; roughly 60% are black and 40% are white. There is also a small but significant community of people who are of Portuguese descent, from the Azores.

Bermuda is a semi-autonomous, self-governing colony. It is a member of the British Commonwealth of Nations. Its international interests and concerns are handled through the Commonwealth Office in Britain; it is represented at the United Nations through Britain and this same link automatically secures channels of representation for the islands at meetings convened by the various UN agencies, as well as many other international forums.

Since the Constitutional Conference of 1968, Bermudians have held control over their own affairs except in the areas of foreign affairs, internal security and external defence. These latter two areas come under the direction of a resident Governor appointed by Her Majesty the Queen. The Bermuda Police Force and the Bermuda Regiment are two local agencies which represent these spheres of his control. The Governor serves as the Queen's representative and his tenure of office continues only as long as Her Majesty wishes. Even in that, however, Bermudians can exert some influence and should they have just cause to seek his removal from office, then Britain is most unlikely to deny such a request. (This did actually happen in 1983 when Governor Sir Richard Posnett was permanently recalled to London following the considerable local displeasure which his Governorship had generated.)

The Bermuda Parliament is organised along very traditional lines and is very similar to the British Parliament, upon which the local structure is based. The Lower House, known as the House of Assembly, consists of forty Members of Parliament, each elected through a general election. These MPs represent twenty island-wide constituencies and each is expected to remain in office until voted out in a subsequent election, unless he or she chooses to retire before that time. During sessions, members meet once a week on a Friday and discuss the multifarious business of that day. Meetings are held in the Sessions House (built in 1817) on Parliament Hill in Hamilton, and are open to the public.

The Upper House is known as The Senate. Here sit eleven Senators. Five of the members are appointed by the Governor, acting on the advice of the Premier; three by the Governor, acting on the advice of the Leader of the Opposition; and three by the Governor, at his own discretion. They discuss items received from the Lower House and final assent from the Senate is usually required for all legislation. The Senate is also a forum through which any topic may be aired and it is often the source for

A member of the Bermuda Police Force directing the traffic from his 'bird-cage'.
(BERMUDA TOURISM)

ideas which are subsequently raised in the Lower House. It is, however, not a parliamentary body elected by the general public. Its members are individually appointed and they serve entirely at the pleasure of those who originally nominated them for the office.

Since the early 1960s, Bermuda has enjoyed a party political system of government. The first party to be formed officially was the Progressive Labour Party (PLP), in 1962. It was followed by the United Bermuda Party (UBP) in 1963, and by the National Liberal Party (NLP), in 1985. The Bermuda Democratic Party (BDP) enjoyed a short life in the late 1960s, but was rejected at the only election it ever fought and promptly sank into oblivion.

Since 1968, the UBP has held the majority of seats in the Lower House and has therefore formed all successive Governments. Its first leader was Sir Henry Tucker (1968 – 71). In his wake have come the following Premiers: Sir Edward Richards

The Sessions House on Parliament Hill in Hamilton. (MICHAEL BOURNE)

(1971 – 75); Sir John Sharpe (1975 – 77); Sir David Gibbons (1977 – 82); the Honourable John W.D. Swan (1982 –).

The leader of the party winning a simple majority during a general election is automatically named to serve as Premier. He is ceremoniously sworn-in by the Governor. Bermudians are responsible for all other aspects affecting the running of the country. The Premier governs mainly through the power of the Cabinet — his own hand-chosen inner circle of politicians. Each holds the title of 'Minister' and the Premier delegates to each the authority to manage various aspects of daily life. There are Ministries to implement the Government's policies towards transport, education, labour and home affairs, tourism, the environment, works and housing, health and social services, youth and sport, finance, community and cultural affairs . . . and so on. The Premier is free to create new Ministries as he/she thinks appropriate, or to abolish those deemed to be redundant. The Cabinet is collectively referred to as the Executive branch of the Government.

Like the Premier, each Minister is a political figure committed to implementing the policies of the ruling party, as they apply to his or her specific Ministry. Also, like that of the Premier, their positions are not regarded as permanent careers, nor are they necessarily secure. The actual day-to-day affairs of the Ministries themselves are carried out by civil servants. These are not politicians, but professionals appointed by the Civil Service Commission. They are hired to do a permanent job and their positions do not change with the formation of a new Government. Civil servants are expected to serve the country, first and foremost; any personal political persuasions are expected to be secondary to that commitment.

Meetings of the Lower House are chaired by the Speaker. This position is one to

The Cabinet Office and Cenotaph on Hamilton waterfront. (MICHAEL BOURNE)

Camden House, official residence of the Premier. (BERMUDA TOURISM)

which the office-holder is elected by his fellow Members of Parliament. The Upper House, or Senate, is chaired by the President, who has been similarly elected from among his fellow Senators. A Deputy is elected for each House, to cover the eventuality of sickness or unavoidable absence.

Bermudians enjoy universal adult suffrage. Providing that they are Bermudian by birth, or by grant of status, and are over the age of twenty-one, all persons are eligible to vote. British subjects resident in Bermuda prior to 21st May, 1976 also enjoy that right. Parliamentary registration is compulsory and a full voters' list is published annually.

The outcome of this system of Government is Bermuda's reputation as a politically and socially stable country, in which occurrences of civil unrest have been very few throughout its entire history. This reputation has resulted in Bermuda being seen by the international community as a reliable focal point for business, banking, investment and tourism.

| 4 |
A tale of two capitals...

With a total population of just slightly more than 57 000, the Islands of Bermuda have only two towns: Hamilton and St George. In addition to these, there are only three areas which we recognise as being villages: North Village (in Devonshire Parish), Somerset Village (in Sandys) and Flatts Village (in Smith's). The rest of the inhabitants are unevenly scattered across each of the main islands of this mid-Atlantic archipelago; some along the main thoroughfares, others rimming the bays and inlets around the coast.

With so few people Bermuda is somewhat unusual among other countries in that each of its two towns bears the title of 'capital'. Hamilton is undoubtedly the actual capital of Bermuda; it has been the official seat of government for these islands throughout the last two centuries and, as if that were not enough for the sceptics, it is clearly marked as such on all maps. On the other hand, every piece of literature both ancient and modern habitually refers to St George as being 'the old capital', perhaps reflecting some subconscious desire to reinforce permanently the fact that this was indeed the original capital of Bermuda for the first two hundred years of her existence.

Hamilton

Hamilton is geographically situated at virtually the centre of the Bermudas, commanding a position which makes it not only a well-protected port, but also something of a nodal centre for the dominant east-to-west pattern of roadways. Neither of these two factors is purely coincidental, however, for they were the specific reasons behind the selection of the site when it came to relocating the capital at the start of the nineteenth century. Alas! St George did not offer the same potential for the growth and expansion which the local merchants and seafarers of the day were then predicting for the country. And so, in 1815, Hamilton formally became the capital of Bermuda — and St George was discreetly relegated to the has-been rank of 'former capital'.

The city of Hamilton is named after Henry Hamilton, who served as Governor from 1788 until 1794. The buildings are clustered upon the innermost shores of Hamilton Harbour, a large body of water which is favourably protected from the open ocean by a sweeping arc of broken landforms created principally by Ireland, Watford and Boaz Islands. Together, they act as a shield which repels much of the unpredictable anger of the Atlantic and thereby provide a tranquil haven for the yachts, cruise-ships and freighters which regularly berth at the quayside.

By sea, the entrance into Hamilton actually begins about eight miles off the East End of Bermuda, where all vessels begin the cautious manoeuvring which will bring

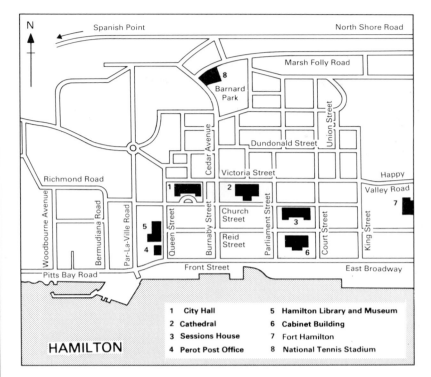

Key to map:

1 City Hall
2 Cathedral
3 Sessions House
4 Perot Post Office
5 Hamilton Library and Museum
6 Cabinet Building
7 Fort Hamilton
8 National Tennis Stadium

HAMILTON

Cruise ship at berth alongside the harbour on Front Street, Hamilton.
(DAVID F. RAINE)

The City Hall on Church Street, Hamilton (DAVID F. RAINE)

them into line with the only safe channel through the coral reefs. Following a series of marker buoys along the North Shore, the boats eventually glide through Two Rock Passage at the mouth of the harbour, and then edge past several smaller islands before coming to rest at the Hamilton docks.

The road which follows the entire length of Hamilton's waterfront is appropriately named Front Street. The majority of the buildings along here date back to the

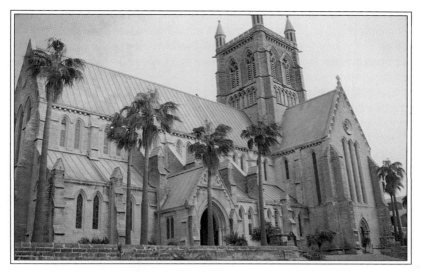

Hamilton Cathedral. (MICHAEL BOURNE)

eighteenth and nineteenth centuries, commercial properties which faced the busy docks where tall clippers and robust brigantines anchored to unload their wares. Today, these same buildings house some of the most distinguished shops in the world, each carrying highly selective merchandise from every continent, except for Antarctica of course. Here the shopper can amble past displays of the best china and porcelain; browse among the most reputable makes of watches and cameras; or look for Shetland

Perot Post Office. (MICHAEL BOURNE)

and Icelandic sweaters, local and overseas artwork, antique and modern furniture. Those wanting to acquire wines and spirits will find several specialist shops on Front Street. Of the local brews, Gosling's 'Black Seal' rum is by far the most celebrated, acting as the main ingredient for many swizzles, as well as Bermuda's most famous drink — the ominous 'Dark and Stormy'.

This international selection of items, with many prices very much competitive with or below those in other countries, tends to be focused upon an area of roughly ten blocks starting on Front Street and then going away from the water up towards Reid, Church and Victoria Streets. These parallel roads are connected by Bermudiana Road, Queen Street, Burnaby Street, Parliament and Court Streets; several interconnecting walkways — Washington Mall, Washington Lane, Walker Arcade and Chancery Lane — all give scope to the extensive range of goods offered by Bermudian shops.

Needless to say, there are many other things to see and do in Hamilton other than shopping. Up on Church Street are the **City Hall** and **Hamilton Cathedral**. The former is simple in design and is a most striking white post-war building, dominated by a 91 foot high tower which contains the Corporation's administrative offices as well as the art gallery which is used for regular exhibitions by the Bermuda Society of Arts. Downstairs, there is a small but well-equipped theatre which is constantly used for productions and recitals by local and visiting companies. On the ground floor, there is a permanent portrait gallery displaying pictures of the city's former Mayors — a succession of Hamilton's most distinguished citizens: the stern, the jowelled, the smiling and the gentle.

Two blocks further east, also on Church Street, is the gothic-style Cathedral, a city landmark which can be clearly seen from far away. Its real name is **Trinity Church** and it stands on the same site as its predecessor, which was sadly destroyed by a raging fire way back in 1884. The present building was begun in 1886 and was eventually consecrated in 1911. The decoration is dominated by characteristically ornate stonework which abounds on both the exterior and interior walls. The figures of Christ and his followers, forming a truly imposing backdrop at the altar, were mainly the work of a local sculptress, the late Ms Billy Lang, arguably the finest stoneworker Bermuda has ever produced.

Down on Queen Street, those with a penchant for history should visit the **Perot Post Office**, the very same one in which Bermuda's nineteenth century post master, W.B. Perot, used to sit meticulously and personally signing all of Bermuda's first stamps, by the flickering light of his lamp. Little did this splendid and diligent gentleman know that one day his handiwork would rank among the rarest collectibles sought by philatelists! The Post Office sits on the edge of **Par-la-Ville Gardens**, the ideal spot for an informal outdoor snack or snooze among carefully manicured flowerbeds and shading trees. Next door is the home for the main branch of the **Bermuda Library**, which has both lending and reference sections. Just inside the entrance, on the ground floor, there is a small but important museum containing some of the country's most important pictures and artefacts, including the original sea-chest and personal

The Bermuda Library, situated in a corner of the Par-La-Ville Gardens.
(MICHAEL BOURNE)

Fort Hamilton from the air. (BERMUDA TOURISM)

lodestone of Sir George Somers. One curiosity among the portraits is the one of Lady Somers — oddly mis-named by the artist as being Winifred, when in truth Sir George was only ever married once, and that was to the youthful Joane Heywood.

On a hillside towards the eastern part of the city limits is **Fort Hamilton**. From the Cathedral, it is about ten minutes' walk. This is another splendid example of one of those defensive forts which were built all over Bermuda in the early nineteenth century. The fort commands a most memorable view of the city itself and Hamilton Harbour right out to the furthermost islands at the tip of Bermuda. Within the fort there are tunnels and an attractively planted moat to explore, as well as a grassy area for eating.

St George

For anyone with a yearning to stroll through narrow streets flanked by the shops and houses of another era altogether, the town of St George provides the perfect setting. Most of the structures in the town have been carefully protected by preservation ordinances which forbid all attempts to update and modernise their appearances. It is therefore important for any first-time visitor to this delightful community to appreciate that the town today is precisely as it is because it has evolved quite naturally during the last four centuries. This is not a reconstructed version of the way things were in the seventeenth century; these are the very same streets along which carts and carriages once rolled, bearing tradesmen and merchants as they went about their

24

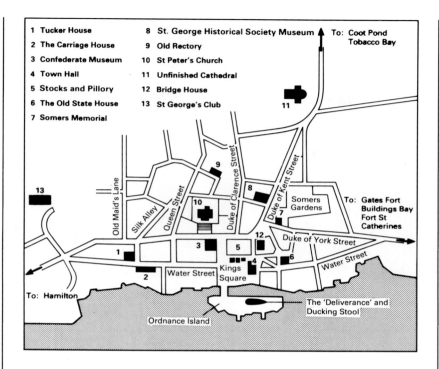

Key to map:

1. Tucker House
2. The Carriage House
3. Confederate Museum
4. Town Hall
5. Stocks and Pillory
6. The Old State House
7. Somers Memorial
8. St. George Historical Society Museum
9. Old Rectory
10. St Peter's Church
11. Unfinished Cathedral
12. Bridge House
13. St George's Club

To: Coot Pond
Tobacco Bay

Old Maid's Lane
Silk Alley
Queen Street
Duke of Clarence Street
Duke of Kent Street
Somers Gardens
To: Gates Fort
Buildings Bay
Fort St Catherines
Duke of York Street
Water Street
Kings Square
Water Street
To: Hamilton
The 'Deliverance' and Ducking Stool
Ordnance Island

daily business. On these very same roadways, wealthy ladies in crinolines and silk passed on their way to the water's edge, doubtless in hopes of greeting their merchant husbands, or of catching the eye of the Captain aboard one of the trading vessels at anchor in the harbour.

Although Sir George Somers and his shipwrecked party lived in and around this particular island between 1609 and 1610, actual settlement of the site did not permanently begin until 1612, when a party of some sixty immigrants led by Richard Moore were landed here from the *Plough*.

From the very outset, it was inevitable that this town would set the tone for everything which might now be described as being 'Bermudian'. It was here that the country's first inhabitants struggled and experimented to develop a style of architecture best suited to the local climate, building materials and living requirements. It was here that they confronted the obvious need to safeguard Bermuda from the wanton destruction of limited natural resources, both on land and in the surrounding ocean. Here they created a port and built warehouses to store the goods they needed to import. They dredged anchorages so that ships might stay and offload cargo and passengers; they formulated laws to govern their daily lives and protect one another against crime. It was here that they tried witches and 'ducked' the gossiping womenfolk! The first-born Bermudians were raised here; the first Parliament was convened here. In St George are the roots of contemporary Bermuda; it furnished the yardstick against which everything else would be measured and checked.

State House, St George. (DAVID F. RAINE)

There are many places to see in this delightful town. The oldest surviving stone building in Bermuda is the **State House**, an angular white structure which is just off **King's Square**. Built during the tenure of Governor Nathaniel Butler in 1620, it was the original seat of local government and was erected at a time when considerable concern was rampant among the townsfolk over the perpetual fire-hazard which the original

St Peter's Church, St George. (MICHAEL BOURNE)

timber and thatched homesteads provided. It pioneered a trend to have all storage and domestic dwellings gradually replaced by more permanent and less dangerous ones constructed from blocks of native limestone. Today it is leased from the Bermuda Government by the Masonic Lodge, St George's — for the annual fee of one solitary peppercorn, publicly handed over during the annual Peppercorn Ceremony.

Tucker House, St George. (DAVID F. RAINE)

Another important building which is always worth a visit is **St Peter's Church**, an imposing building in the town's centre which lays claim to being the oldest continuously used Anglican church in the western hemisphere. Once you have climbed the rather awesome flight of red brick steps at the front, the aroma of cedar permeates all other smells — for this church is lined throughout with cedar, from its beams to the pews and the seventeenth century pulpit. In the ante-room, there is a superb collection of silver chalices and bowls, some presented by English and American dignitaries three hundred years ago. The interior walls of the church are lined with memorials and plaques to commemorate the innumerable souls who have passed away on these shores; a wander among the headstones in the surrounding cemetery is similarly interesting.

Among the many fascinating buildings in St George, four are especially worth visiting. On Water Street there is the **Carriage Museum**, which houses an unusual collection of carriages gathered by the Wilkinson family. Each vehicle has been painstakingly preserved and, for the uninitiated, there is a concise explanatory note giving some general background to each type of carriage. Opposite the museum is **Tucker House** — an authentic early eighteenth century family home in which each room has been carefully re-furnished with appropriate furnishings, portraits and antiques by the Bermuda National Trust. The basement of the house has been carefully converted into St George's leading bookstore — appropriately called 'The Book Cellar'. An officially sanctioned archaeological dig was begun beneath Tucker House in 1988, an on-going project which has subsequently yielded many domestic artefacts from the daily life of the last two hundred and fifty years.

Confederate Museum, St George. (DAVID F. RAINE)

Bridge House, St George. (DAVID F. RAINE)

On the corner of Featherbed Alley and Duke of Kent Street, the St George's Historical Society has converted another private home of similar date into a museum. Like Tucker House, it has been entirely refurnished with period pieces as well as a variety of memorabilia and domestic artefacts either collected by private individuals, or donated through bequests.

Just on the edge of King's Square is the **Confederate Museum**. This contains various pieces of memorabilia highlighting Bermuda's somewhat intriguing trading role during the American Civil War, when St George was often the start of a desperate race by blockade-runners eager to take merchandise through to the beleaguered southern States. The building itself was built in 1699 and was originally the home of Governor Samuel Day. However, with the outbreak of war in 1861 it also became the residence of a Major Norman S. Walker, the chief political agent for the Confederate States, and the man who actually organised the illicit trade with the South, an activity conducted in the dining-rooms and among the shadows of St George's winding streets. It has been estimated that the conflict cost Southerners as much as $3000 million — some of which unquestionably passed through St George.

Governors Alured and William Popple lived at **Bridge House**, just off the main square, as did the celebrated American privateer Bridger Goodrich. This is an enchanting home, now owned by the Bermuda National Trust. Its traditional walled gardens are picturesquely maintained and visitors can get some further idea of early lifestyles by walking up the steps, on to the lower verandah and into rooms on the ground floor. Today the former dining-rooms are used as a unique setting for the **Bridge House Art Gallery and Craft Shop** — Bermuda's main centre for all local arts and crafts.

On Ordnance Island, on the other side of the bridge at King's Square, there is a replica of the *Deliverance*, one of the two vessels originally built in 1609 by the survivors of the shipwrecked *Sea Venture*, using what they could salvage from the wreck. It is managed by the Junior Service League and, for a small fee which goes to charity, anyone can climb aboard and wander around a boat whose original, incredibly, took 120 people safely all the way to the pioneering settlement of Jamestown, Virginia.

St George is also a key shopping area. Most of the major Hamilton stores have branches here and, from many points of view, it is far more enjoyable to shop here where it is considerably less crowded. Furthermore, many of the smaller stores offer very competitive prices on a broad range of merchandise because rents are so much lower in St George than in Hamilton. The two main roads in St George are Water Street and Duke of York Street, each of which is lined with stores. Other shops are located around King's Square and down on Somers Wharf, off Water Street — a delightfully designed shopping complex which offers all manner of clothing and souvenirs, and even a selection of craftwork upstairs in 'Whichcraft'. On adjacent **Hunter's Wharf**, it is worth popping into 'Bermuda Beauty Crafts', to watch straw bags being made, and then calling into the shop next door which prints tee-shirts.

Bermuda's two towns offer comparable amenities, but entirely different surroundings. But then this is the way one might expect it to be — after all, one is the capital of today whilst the other was the capital of yesteryear.

Left: *The replica of the* Deliverance *on Ordnance Island.* (G.W. LENNOX)

|5|
A sun that shines
on things that grow...

For much of the year, Bermuda enjoys a warm and sunny sub-tropical climate characterised by constantly high humidity and temperatures which rarely leave the mid- to upper-eighties. The seas which wash her shores remain unfailingly tepid. There is almost no significant change to this daily pattern and not even the nights become cool. In summer, the only respite from the heat lies in the short sharp showers which seem to fall from cloudless skies, momentarily depositing a shining glaze over the landscape. All too soon this evaporates and the much needed fresh water is gone again. During the winter months, when the North Atlantic becomes wracked by passing storm systems, the weather becomes less certain and the islands are intermittently wafted by alternating gusts and breezes which reduce the air temperature into the sixties and lower seventies.

Such a warm, damp climate is naturally conducive to the growth of a rich, luscious vegetation. Devoid of conventional seasons, the countryside is forever green. Carefully-trimmed hedges line the roadsides, each covered with a multicoloured display of exotic blooms; nearby, palm trees rise above the dry-stone walls encircling a banana patch.

Blue plumbago. (DAVID F. RAINE)

Yellow and white hibiscus. (DAVID F. RAINE)

Not for Bermuda are the browning death-throes of trees in fall, nor the starkness of naked bushes shivering into winter. Bermuda offers its own colourful backdrop during every month of the year and there are always flowers blossoming somewhere, like the pink and peach hibiscus, purple morning glory, white oleander, blue plumbago or the red berries of Mexican pepper.

White oleander. (DAVID F. RAINE)

However, the vegetation which flourishes throughout Bermuda today is not the same as that which so generously greeted her original settlers. Sadly, of course, such is the globally repeated reality of progress. The North American undergrowth, which Champlain hacked through whilst portaging into the interior, has given way to concrete high-rises; the oak forests of England have long since surrendered to the denuded, rolling scenery of the grassy Downs. So too has Bermuda's natural vegetation changed.

In other countries, it seems easy to blame serious environmental abuses on some remote historic excess, such as overzealous axemen trying to feed the wooden needs of the neighbourhood boatbuilders and explorers; or we may choose to point accusing fingers at the financial greed of inconsiderate land developers who have long since passed away. In Bermuda, however, no such excuses are needed to explain the catastrophic changes which have occurred to the natural vegetation of these islands. Instead, it is almost completely due to a miniscule scale insect named *Carulaspis minima* (previously recorded as *C. visci*) — the perpetrator of a blight which, during the late 1940s, successfully managed to destroy an estimated 80% of Bermuda's indigenous cedar forest. So extensive was the impact of this fatal infestation that it was not until the 1970s that our endemic *Juniperus bermudiana* began to make a recovery, and a campaign to commence planting seeds 'for the next generation' was subsequently launched. (In the interim, the barren landscape was hastily replanted with the fast-growing casuarina.)

Bermuda was once a dense forest in which cedars and palmettoes vied for dominance. Low-lying buttonwoods crawled along the coastline, their roots delving deeply into every available crevice until they were firmly anchored into the pitted limestone rock. Yellowwoods grew everywhere, whilst vines such as the small passion-flower and Virginia creeper dangled from branches. Further inland, maidenhair ferns thrived in the dark dampness of caves, whilst others burst from the warm wet bed of decaying leaves which carpeted the areas adjacent to the mangrove swamps and marshes. In drier areas, the prickly pear cactus was not only prolific, but also very popular for its fruit, which was used for food and also as a dye.

By the end of the seventeenth century, human settlement had spread from one tip of Bermuda to the other, leaving in its wake a trail of fields, gardens and buildings. Hedges, walls and pathways began to thin the forests and neatly-pruned rows of bushes were everywhere replacing the less formal, natural undergrowth. Economic necessity, however, demanded that the early Bermudians should immediately replace each uprooted plant with another, preferably something which would prove to have more productive benefits. By 1650 several botanical excursions had already been made to the Caribbean and along the Eastern Seaboard, with the specific intention of starting the experimental introduction of various forms of plant-life into the fledgling colony. Tobacco and cotton were planted, as were mulberries for silkworms, with the hopes each might form the basis for an entire industry. Herbs, spices and flowers soon followed, as did fiddlewoods, allspice and Surinam cherry.

Thus began the tradition of importing shrubs, trees, vines and bulbs into Bermuda, a practice which has made these islands today an extensive garden in which different plants from widely scattered parts of the world have become uniquely naturalised.

An Easter lily. (DAVID F. RAINE)

During any trip around Bermuda, even the most casual observer is likely to be struck by the colourful profusion of oleander and hibiscus.

Oleander is used extensively in hedges and as a windbreak; if left uncut, bushes may grow up to twenty feet in height. Originally a cultivated plant from the Orient, it became popular in Mediterranean areas and now readily grows quite prolifically throughout the West Indies. Pink and white are the most common hues in Bermuda — the former, when doubled in salmon pink, is locally known as 'Paget oleander'. For all of its beauty, oleander is poisonous to animals and can even be fatal to humans.

Hibiscus is also used for hedges. An estimated 150 types have been identified throughout the world, although in Bermuda the 'China Rose' variety is by far the most prevalent. It was apparently brought up from the West Indian islands of Jamaica and Cuba. Local varieties come in shades of pink, red, peach, white and yellow; the flowers may be single or double. Another type (*Malvariscus arboreus*)often seen in gardens is the 'Sleepy hibiscus' — a brilliant red variety which appears to be forever drooping

Palm Grove Gardens, where a variety of the Palm species can be seen.
(BERMUDA TOURISM)

and unopened, a disposition which has resulted in the caustic nickname of 'Scotman's purse'! This particular genus is actually Mexican in origin however.

During the traditional months of spring, Bermudian gardens are dominated by the delightful fragrance of Easter lilies. Whole parks and fields seem to glow with the long trumpet-like blooms, whilst even hillsides may offer wild and random sprays of whiteness, marking places where bulbs have been casually scattered in the past. Bermuda once exported these lilies in vast quantities and still does so on a far more limited scale. It is still a custom that Bermudian lilies are sent to the Queen at Easter-time, on behalf of the people of these islands.

Palm trees may also be seen all over Bermuda. The only truly endemic species is the thick-trunked palmetto, which was once used for a variety of purposes ranging from rope-making to weaving; for a while, our palmetto hats were very fashionable on the streets of London. The berries were even fermented into a highly potent drink called 'Bibby' — a liquid which soon had the distinction of becoming the first intoxicating beverage to be banned in Bermuda!

Perhaps the most easily recognised palm is the taller and more slender coconut palm which grows naturally along the sandy coastal regions. Local varieties, however, seldom produce an edible fruit, apparently because Bermuda's cool winters occur during a crucial period of their growth, and the pod frequently fails to develop fully. The same applies to the fruit of the shorter date palm, which really requires the consistent dry heat of its native North Africa in order to reach fruition effectively. Equally elegant is the even taller royal palm which became popular during the last century for lining the driveways and paths of some of the grander estates. It is in distinct contrast to the squat sago palm (*Cycas revoluta*), which rarely exceeds a stubby four feet in height but whose central cap of bright orange seeds has a distinctive charm all of its own. This is, however, not a true palm, but a cycad, as its Latin name implies.

One of the more visually striking plants is the bougainvillea. Named after an eminent French navigator, this woody vine originated in Brazil but was successfully introduced into Bermuda through cuttings brought from the Caribbean. It is particularly distinctive for its spectacular sprays of vivid purple and red flowers, hanging in bulky clusters along fences or among dead trees. Also found along walls and among dead cedars is the trailing succulent, night-blooming cereus. Because it really does bloom during the night, there is something ironic in the fact that its enormous and exotic cream-coloured flowers — often attaining a diameter of ten inches — are less noticeable than many smaller flowers. Two out of the three types of cereus are however extremely fragrant and you couldn't miss them! But the third type (*Hylocereus undatus*) is more inconspicuous. Many are those who have unknowingly strolled past it in the darkness.

Plumbago is another trailing plant which grows throughout Bermuda. It weaves its way among hedges, or is decoratively fastened to trellises alongside house walls, and produces very delicate light-blue flowers during much of the year. It grows best in protected areas and is pleasantly ornamental. The tamarisk is quite different. Not only is its dishevelled appearance far less attractive, but it tends to thrive in a far more exposed environment. Towards the end of the last century it was used extensively as a windbreak along sections of the North Shore — a function which primarily accounts for its widespread popularity up to the present.

Another completely functional import is the full range of trees in the citrus family. A regular component of Bermuda's vegetation for two centuries, they are found island-wide. All are domesticated rather than wild. Grapefruit, orange, tangelo, lemon and lime can be seen in many private gardens. When crushed in the hand, the leaves exude the same pleasing smell as the actual fruit; the blossoms which precede the fruit give off a splendid fragrance. As is the case with avocado trees, an insufficient amount of fruit is produced to make a significant contribution to the country's food chain.

With a continuously expanding population and the inherent pressure which the demand for housing has placed on Bermuda's landscape, the undisturbed areas of natural vegetation have diminished rapidly in the last twenty years. Major marshes such as those in Paget and Devonshire Parishes continue to provide a vital link with the way things used to be. The Government parks help to preserve other unspoilt open spaces.

The uniqueness of Bermuda's vegetation does not lie exclusively in those small and isolated pockets which have eluded man's interference. It perhaps manifests itself best in the truly unique manner in which plants from all over the world have become naturalised in Bermuda, producing an extravagant cornucopia in which pawpaw, Norfolk Island pine and poinsettia grow comfortably side by side; where geraniums grow as rapidly as weeds, and where aloes rise through beds of nasturtiums.

|6|
An abundance of
limited wildlife

Although Bermuda remained unpopulated until the seventeenth century, this should not be taken to infer that these islands were completely bereft of all life-forms. The seas were once teeming with fish, turtles and dolphins; lizards scurried among the palms and vines. In the trees and along the cliffs a multitude of birds warbled a daily chorus of chirps and caws. And, every so often, the dense undergrowth reverberated with the thunderous pounding of marauding wild hogs.

The earliest accounts of Bermuda's wildlife date back to the 1500s. The island's namesake, Juan de Bermudez, drifted through these waters in 1505 and remarked upon the abundance of sea-life which could be spotted with every wave. In 1543, the Portuguese mariner, Gonzalo Fernandez d'Orviedo y Valdes, paused here for a short while and wrote delightfully about the 'strive and combat' which he witnessed in these treacherous seas with flying fish being chased by giltheads from below, and cormorants from above. However, accounts such as these are inevitably very subjective sketches, often based upon the random experiences of sailors who briefly stepped ashore and stayed long enough to have only a quick glimpse of the area, before hastily racing back to the safety of their ships.

Perhaps the first in-depth description of an encounter with Bermuda's wildlife is one dated 1603. In December of that year a fleet of five ships under the command of Don Luis de Cordova was badly battered by a severe storm just to the south of Bermuda. All but one of the boats sank without further trace of either man or planks. The fifth was fortunately washed through the reefs and the survivors remained here long enough to effect repairs and draw a map of these uninhabited isles, before continuing on their interrupted journey back to Europe. But the shipwreck is not actually the part of their story for which the survivors are generally remembered. Rather, the single aspect of their trials and tribulations which is most often quoted centres upon a crew member who was reputedly attacked by the ferocious local wildlife.

Among the sailors there was a negro named Venturilla. According to the tale, one night he was wandering through the woods of Bermuda carrying a flickering lantern to light his way. Suddenly, he let out the most horrendous of screams and yelled that he was being attacked by 'devilles'; the screeching attracted the attention of his shipmates who, having approached close enough to establish that the hapless Venturilla was indeed being viciously assaulted by a horde of something, promptly abandoned both loyalty and their mate, and headed out to sea in long boats! In fact, Venturilla's light had merely attracted a host of cahows, each rising to protect its nest from the unexpected intruder, and when the timid sailors eventually plucked up enough

A Cahow. (DAVID WINGATE)

courage to return to the scene, there sat the perplexed seaman encircled by dozens of stunned birds.

The first detailed accounts of Bermuda's original wildlife were in the 1610 tomes written independently by Silvanus Jourdain and William Strachy, both of the *Sea Venture*. Squatting on a rock somewhere in the vicinity of where **St David's Lighthouse** now stands, Strachy painstakingly quilled the results of ten months' observations concerning the land, air and sea creatures which he had noted. Coupled with the work of Jourdain, it provides a full listing of Bermuda's native wildlife.

Both agree that fish were so prolific that they swarmed everywhere around the shores. Rockfish, pilchards and mullet were fully in evidence, as were bonito, angelfish, hogfish, bream, snappers, stingrays and sharks. Offshore they occasionally saw whales and even sometimes a solitary swordfish hunting beyong the reefs; among the rocks they spotted various eels and a variety of crabs and lobsters. Oysters, too, were very common, as were various kinds of clams and shellfish. Clearly, these waters were adequately and naturally stocked with sufficient sea-life to satisfy even the emptiest of stomachs.

The observers were equally jubilant about the quantities and varieties of birds which they discovered at different times of the year. Their lists include: buntings, bitterns, sparrows, teals, crows, hawks, coots, cormorants, owls, moorhen and plovers. There were egrets and cahows everywhere, as well as flocks of robins, terns, tropicbirds, herons and even swans. Jourdain mentions that often the birds were so dense and tame that they could be felled with a stick by anyone walking through the trees. Eggs

A humpback whale. (DAVID WINGATE)

were there for the taking, as nests filled every hollow in the ground and every crevice in the cliffs.

As now, Bermuda was without any venomous or dangerous animals. There never were any poisonous spiders or snakes on these islands and the first records of disease-spreading vermin such as rats do not appear until 1618. In their place there were turtles basking on the beaches; silk spiders harmlessly spinning webs in the mulberry bushes and a large number of bats flapping in and out of the caves at night.

The most enigmatic of Bermuda's native wildlife was surely the hog, also variously referred to as either swine, pig, sow or boar. There is no doubt that they once roamed these islands freely and in vast quantities; they appear in all of the early narratives and were a vital part of everyone's diet. Sir George Somers mentions that his hunters would sometimes capture as many as fifty per week; many more were kept in corrals and then slaughtered as the kitchen required.

The abundance of hogs on an island so far from the mainland forests where they customarily roamed is an apparent oddity of nature. Their prevalence in Bermuda, however, is easily explained. It is common practice for many explorers to deposit food caches along their routes, so that in the event of some unforeseen emergency they have supplies to fall back upon. The seafarers of the Elizabethan age were no exception and for the Portuguese in particular it was very much a traditional safeguard. After his discovery of Newfoundland in 1583, Sir Humphrey Gilbert directed his small fleet to make for the island of Sablon, where they expected to find ample stocks of fresh swine, known to have been left there for that very purpose by Portuguese sailors some thirty years earlier. Bermuda's own rampaging wild hogs unquestionably owe their origins to this same thoughtful consideration, and today are perpetually commemorated on the one cent coin — hence 'hog penny'. In the late nineteenth century, Governor Lefroy discovered the near-perfect skull of one of these early residents; another similar specimen was unearthed in Southampton Parish in January 1981.

As the human population increased, inevitably and sadly the various forms of Bermuda's original wildlife diminished. The carefree turtles were highly favoured for their meat and were easily gaffed from rowing boats. They were baked and roasted; their oil was used in lamps, for cooking and even mixed with mud to produce a building plaster. Their eggs were taken as liberally as were the eggs of birds, until the natural stocks of adults and young began to diminish. The vulnerable cahows, in fact, were all but eaten into extinction — indeed, until the middle of the twentieth century it was believed that they truly were extinct.

Man's subsequent encroachment into the natural environment has drastically diminished the original habitat of most of Bermuda's wildlife, and the deliberate introduction of toads and kiskadees has artificially reduced the natural levels of their prey and severely upset the delicate balance of nature. The global problems caused by polluting the seas has been witnessed by a disturbing drop in the catches of local fishermen. No longer do the fish swarm eagerly round the feet of casual waders, as they did in the days of Silvanus Jourdain; the extensive use of pots, and over-fishing, have only served to emphasise the world-wide depletion of fish and various sea mammals. The catching of turtles and conch is specifically prohibited in order to let

The Bermuda skink. (DAVID WINGATE)

The Bermuda Aquarium. (DAVID RAINE)

their numbers recover, and many other species of molluscs and lobsters are protected by seasonal restrictions. Whales, once a minor industry here, are no longer hunted. The harpoons, oil cauldrons and knives have been rightfully relegated to display spaces in the Maritime Museum.

Even if there are fewer fish in the sea and we no longer face the danger of being attacked by wild hogs or swarms of diving cahows, there is much comfort to be had from the state of the wildlife which does continue to exist on these islands of Bermuda. Hundreds of migratory birds visit here during the course of each year; silk spiders still leisurely spin their cocoon-like webs throughout the country.

Various projects, diligently monitored under the auspices of the Government, have recently produced some very encouraging results in turtle breeding. For several years young hatchlings have been released from local beaches and hopes are high that eventually they will return to the same spot as breeding adults. Each year, the Bermuda Zoological Society arranges trips out to sea in order to watch pods of humpback whales blowing their way past our shores. Many of the original recordings of the 'songs' of humpback whales were made off Bermuda, by Dr Roger Payne.

Another success story lies with the breeding of the cahow. Once formally registered as an extinct species of bird, specimens were located on some of the smaller islands off Bermuda's East End. Now, under the personal and watchful eye of Bermudian ornithologist David Wingate, their numbers continue to increase steadily and there is every hope that they will become fully established once more. In the interim, their breeding sites remain a justifiably closed secret.

The 'Bluebird Society' continues to claim dramatic increases in the population of that particular bird, and mounts an ongoing campaign to encourage householders to install breeding boxes in their gardens. Bats, owls and night herons may still be spotted darting or gliding through the skies at dusk; the colourful parrotfish can be watched from most rocky shorelines as they rise and fall with the incoming waves, nibbling at growths on the coral heads.

There is a very earnest desire to preserve whatever remains of Bermuda's natural environment, and the multifarious forms of wildlife which inhabit it. Parks have been set aside; there are several nature reserves which attract transient birds as well as native residents. In 1988, local conservationists were internationally acknowledged for successfully breeding the island's own endemic lizard, known as the Bermuda skink. Like others, this programme comes under the direction of staff at the **Bermuda Aquarium** and remains the only record of captive breeding for this endangered species anywhere in the world.

Perhaps Bermuda's natural wildlife has been severely depleted since those distant days when William Strachy sat on a rock making notes, or when the shipwrecked Venturilla had to fend off cahows by swinging a stick. By legislating for land-use and strictly controlling ongoing development of the islands, Bermudians have managed to curb the tide of extinction which once faced many of the natural inhabitants. There is every hope that stocks will again rise closer to their original levels.

| 7 |
Bermudian Architecture

There is something very different about Bermudian architecture, something which becomes apparent the first time that you look down at these islands from the air. Other than noticing the turquoise water and reefs, the eye is immediately drawn to the white roofs which are scattered across the landscape, like confetti tossed by an over-zealous guest. For those arriving by sea, the reaction of the eminent nineteenth century American photographer Edith Ross Parker, as she saw Bermuda early one morning in 1899, remains forever apt. To her the houses looked like tiny flecks of white paper which someone had sparingly sprinkled amidst the luscious green and brown vegetation.

Whether first seen by air or by sea, Bermudian architecture is indeed quite unlike that found elsewhere. Certainly the houses are distinctive for their white roofs and pastel coloured walls, but their shape and design are also unusual for the manner in which various features have been borrowed from distant shores and modified to suit local conditions.

Three main factors have moulded what is universally recognised as 'Bermudian architecture' today: available building materials, the need for fresh water and the specific demands of Bermuda's climate.

As elsewhere, the island's first builders used whatever materials they could conveniently find. Cedar and palmetto were used extensively to make temporary cabins and shelters, but for more permanent dwellings they soon began to utilise the native coralline limestone which abounds everywhere. It was a rock which could be easily excavated and sawn into blocks, but its often fragile and crumbly texture necessitated that it be hewn into thick slabs, rather than small bricks. This automatically produced a style of house based upon very sturdy walls, frequently a foot or more in thickness.

Lacking either the grey slates of Europe or the wooden shingles of North America, the settlers carefully cut the limestone rock into thin slices and used it as a roofing material. The 'slates' were laid in such a manner as to produce the effect of shallow descending steps and created a solid capping to each house. Such rooftops had a dual advantage. They not only offered solid protection from the elements, but also satisfied another basic requirement. When sealed and painted with a wash of lime, they proved to be the perfect means for catching and purifying rainwater. Devoid of any significant surface water — even the brackish pond and marsh waters have an inevitably high saline content — freshwater supplies were, and still are, of paramount importance. The rooftops became the most obvious catchment areas. Rainwater falls on to the roof and is guided down into storage tanks. Modern homes have tanks built underneath the main structure; older houses had a barrel-vaulted water tank built on to the side of the house and rainwater was guided into it via a system of pipes.

A typical Bermudian home showing the famous white roofs and pastel coloured walls. (MICHAEL BOURNE)

Water trapped and stored by this method is naturally fresh and remains as cool as that caught in an underground cavern. Rooftops and tanks continue to be the sole method we have for catching and storing domestic water.

Climate was the third factor which Bermuda's architects had to confront immediately. The North Atlantic is notorious for its winter storms — indeed, even the good Sir Walter Raleigh advised his fleets to steer clear of the turbulent winter waters near 'The Bermoothes'. Additionally, these otherwise tranquil islands also lie along the summer hurricane track. Bermudian architecture consequently developed traits which were responsive to potential damage from severe storms. The builders opted to anticipate the worse aspects of the weather and adopted principles which were quite different from those incorporated in buildings throughout the West Indies. Their perceptive wisdom carries itself into the present; as the world watches the destructive power of storms virtually every year somewhere in the Caribbean, rarely does such devastation strike Bermudians or their homes.

The basic format for local houses was necessarily solid and functional, and these same traits were incorporated into the various features which give each dwelling its own individual personality and character. An early decision was made, for example, not to have wide eaves around each building; although these are used extensively to the south, as a source of shade, their vulnerability to ripping winds was soon apparent. In Bermuda, therefore, the eaves are narrow and for shade we include an open porch into the overall design of the house — producing, in effect, an open windowless room from which we may all enjoy the benefits of outdoor living, without

45

The buttery at Springfield. (DEPARTMENT OF TOURISM, BERMUDA)

the dangers. These are thoughtfully located on that side of the house which will offer maximum shade, whilst simultaneously reaping the fullest benefits of the breezes which blow on to these shores for most of the year.

Even chimneys were built with the weather in mind. Houses, in fact, were often quite deliberately orientated so as to have the external chimney breast constructed as an extra support to the wall facing the prevailing southerly winds. Delicate chimney pots are still unheard of here; instead, firm limestone slabs are mounted at the top of each chimney.

In considering how to embellish their buildings, Bermudian architects chose mainly to ignore the use of delicate woodwork. Instead, they favoured chunky gable-ends and then tastefully decorated them with the graceful curves found in many of the churches of colonial Mexico. They sometimes erected triangular pediments above entrance-ways, and supported these with mock Doric pillars to mimic the grandeur of ancient Greece. Gates were flanked by massive, square stone posts, often surmounted by huge balls of carved limestone; in some cases, similarly crude rock shapes were positioned on roof ends, in imitation of the highly-decorative glazed finials used on traditional oriental rooftops.

They added shutters to the windows in the style known as 'jalousies', which hinge at the top and keep the sun at bay when open, and offer protection from fierce winds when closed.

One of the most singularly distinctive structures in Bermudian architecture is the buttery. Designed for use in days long before the advent of refrigeration, the butteries

Left: *A fine example of an old family house built in the neo-classical design.*
(MICHAEL BOURNE)

47

represent an inventive attempt to keep foodstuffs cool. It is really an outhouse, of sorts, with a high roof shaped like a pyramid. Built away from the main house, the buttery exploited the principle that warm air would rise into the pointed ceiling and leave cooler air in the lower portion of the room, where the food was stored. They were even built in such a way that each wall was slatted to allow air to drift into the interior without exposing it to any direct sunlight. Butteries can still be found in the grounds of some of the larger properties. The best survivor is undoubtedly the well-photographed buttery at **Springfield** in Somerset. It is not too uncommon to find the buttery shape still being adopted to form an entrance area into private homes.

Construction techniques and building materials have changed considerably during the last four centuries but contemporary domestic architecture in Bermuda still bears all of the same basic characteristics which have been passed down by generations of local builders and architects. Each house still catches its own water on a neatly white-washed roof; our homes remain thick-walled and sturdy enough to resist most onslaughts from the elements. We still have shutters for windows and limestone slabs instead of chimney pots.

|8|
The legendary Bermuda Triangle

There was a time when Bermuda was universally thought of for its clear waters and pink beaches; as the playground of the rich and famous; as a paradise on earth. In the last couple of decades, however, mention of these islands also invariably conjures up mysterious images relating to the 'Bermuda Triangle'.

The origin of the term itself is usually credited to a writer named Vincent Gaddis, who first used it in a magazine article published in the 1950s to describe some strange events which had occurred in the area. However, much of the popular mystique relating to the so-called 'Bermuda Triangle' is actually the result of the imaginative writings

A map of the Bermuda Triange illustrating the disappearances of ships and planes in the area. (TOPHAM PICTURE LIBRARY)

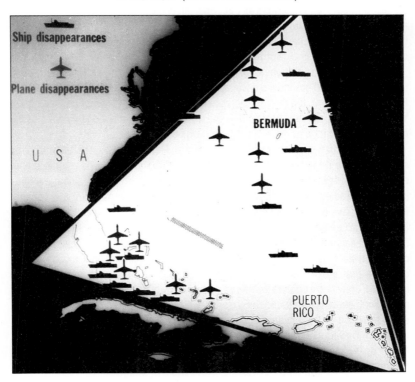

of Adi-Kent Jeffrey. It was this lady who somehow managed to embroider fact with fiction attractively and produced fanciful images of galleons being sucked into swirling watery vortexes and then being dragged beneath the angry seas. It was primarily her writings, published in 1973, which stimulated subsequent illustrators to produce sketches of awesome hands reaching from churning waters, whilst the agonised faces of deckhands pleaded hopelessly at rolling black clouds and mountainous waves.

If those stories pitted sailors against the evil faces of the elements, then we must credit John Wallace Spencer with perpetuating even more unusual notions. It was he who, in 1969, conceived the existence of a graveyard for derelict ships, all fastened to drifting anchorages in the matted seaweeds of the Sargasso Sea. To him we may also attribute the greatest responsibility for some of the slightly more peculiar comings and goings within this region, for it was Spencer who submitted that the probable explanation for the 'limbo of the lost' was in another dimension altogether — that extra-terrestrials were culling this portion of the Atlantic Ocean for scientific research purposes. In 1974, both Charles Berlitz and Richard Winer wrote books which seemingly supported these and similar theories. Berlitz, in fact, even resurrected the 'lost continent of Atlantis' and injected it into the mystery, as another possible explanation.

Once again, illustrators in the popular press obliged with detailed pictures of descending spaceships beaming earthbound lights, and battered galleons entangled in sargasso weed, their ghostly crews trapped in an endless time warp. Even the highly-respected Bermudian authoress Terry Tucker mentioned in one of her books the case of an abandoned boat named *Eliza Ann* drifting into nineteenth century Bermuda with only skeletons on board. But her evidence is extremely thin.

What then is the truth behind all of these writings? There can be no doubt at all that the unexplained has indeed occurred in the vast area of the Atlantic which extends from Bermuda, down to the West Indies and up along the North American mainland. Yachts, galleons, aircraft, submarines and tankers have unquestionably entered the region, lost contact and never been found again.

Among the many instances is that of the British Royal Navy frigate *Atalanta*. This superb tall ship departed from Bermuda on 1st February, 1880, with a complement of 107 naval officers and cadets after completing an intensive sail-training exercise in the West Indies. As Bermudians watched her sails slip gently over the horizon, none could have realised that neither the boat nor its crew would ever be seen again. Even after an extensive search of the ocean by support ships of the Royal Navy and others, not a scrap of evidence was ever found to explain the strange disappearance of the *Atalanta*. In absolute dismay, an official Board of Enquiry in London was forced to conclude that despite a relentless search of the area, a thorough examination of individual crew backgrounds and a complete survey of the vessel's structural plans, no logical explanation could be offered which might account for the strange disappearance of the *Atalanta*.

Equally bewildering was the fate of a 'Tudor' aircraft owned by British South American Airlines, which seemingly vanished as it was about to make a landing approach to Bermuda on 29th January, 1948. Having completed its trip from England to

Bermudian waters at their calmest, making it hard to believe the horror stories of the Bermuda Triangle. (BERMUDA TOURISM)

the Azores without any hitches, the 'Star Tiger' took to the air once more and headed towards Bermuda; there it would off-load some passengers and then refuel prior to departure for the West Indies. At 10.30 p.m. on 30th January, the pilot contacted the control tower at Kindley Field in Bermuda with final confirmation of their position; he reported his altitude, fuel status and the weather conditions. It was the last communication ever received from the ill-fated aircraft. An extensive search was immediately organised, but no wreckage was ever located.

If that was not troubling enough, almost one year later its sister plane 'Star Ariel' suffered an equally baffling fate. On 19th January, 1949, she took off from Bermuda and headed towards The Bahamas. Less than an hour into the flight southwards, the pilot thanked Bermuda control and indicated that he was going to transfer radio contact to Nassau immediately. It was his last message. Again, an immediate search-and-rescue produced no clues as to what had happened to the ill-fated 'Star Ariel'; all on board were lost.

An official Board of Enquiry was obliged to admit in the conclusion of its lengthy report that no explanation had been found to account for the loss of either aircraft. All similar models were withdrawn from service and for some years after these events BSAA solved the unfathomable and mysterious problem simply by not operating flights along these air routes.

There are countless other tales to excite and mystify a legion of readers: yachts being recovered with no one on board; the French submarine *Surcouf* which submerged off Bermuda at 3.00 p.m. on 12th February, 1942 and headed southwards, forever. Then there is the factual story of the entire flight of 5 US Navy *Avengers* which took off on a regular training mission into this area in 1945 — and never returned. Nor for that matter did one of the search planes promptly sent aloft to find them.

Perhaps one of the most bizarre episodes of all was not an unexplainable disappearance, but the actual exorcism of the 'Bermuda Triangle' by the Reverend Donald Omond, in 1978. With the full knowledge and approval of his Archbishop and the Church hierarchy, this Anglican clergyman with a proven record for conducting exorcisms arrived in Bermuda and undertook his devil-defying work from the balcony of a major hotel along the South Shore. He then scurried to the nearby beach at Horseshoe Bay and completed his efforts by physically standing in the waves and purging the waters. As he sprawled exhausted on his bed, the priest cautiously remarked that only time would tell whether he had been successful in ridding the 'Bermuda Triangle' of its evil forces.

Where is the line between reality and myth? What are the indisputable facts and what is fanciful and speculative elaboration? Certainly boats, planes and people have entered the seas and air in this particular portion of the North Atlantic and have either disappeared altogether, or have had unusual experiences. We might, however, also take into account the fact that the so-called 'Bermuda Triangle' covers thousands and thousands of square miles. It is a body of water so vast that boats still pass within miles of one another in full daylight without ever actually noticing each other. The waters are so incredibly deep that even as recently as 1984 the *Marques* suddenly sank without trace 60 miles off Bermuda, whilst actively competing in a well-monitored Tall Ships Race to Halifax. A handful of survivors individually agreed that an intense squall rose in the night and completely overpowered them within minutes.

It might be reasonable to accept that the region of the so-called 'Bermuda Triangle' is one which has always been frequented by a very high density of sea and air traffic. From the earliest times when galleons began routinely passing through here in convoys, right up to the present time of constantly-expanding trade between Europe, North America and the Caribbean, ships and planes have repeatedly crossed its waterways and air-space. There have been accidents and tragedies, many admittedly unexplained. Comparative statistics, however, indicate that the overwhelming majority of those of us who regularly cross this portion of the Atlantic can do so with less concern than those who drive along the Inter-state highways of the United States on holiday weekends.

| 9 |
Traditions

Anyone who really wants to know this country, who wants to delve deeply into its soul and feel its pulse, can find no more effective way than by fingering through an index of its traditions. Traditions enable us to watch the past and the present living side by side; they let us peel away the veneer and see what actually lies beyond.

With a social history reaching back into the early seventeenth century, Bermudian life is inevitably filled with a spectrum of traditions. They encompass sports, architecture and gardening; they embrace styles of clothing, modes of travel and peculiarities of speech. Some are expressed in the pomp and pageantry of a parade; others are revealed in a simple greeting from a stranger in the street, for Bermudians enjoy a reputation for friendliness. We even have a tradition of using nicknames, so that local newspapers, court records and telephone books are generously peppered with references to such noteworthies as 'Snuffy' Smith, 'Rubberneck' Trott, 'Toes', 'Chips', 'Hector', 'Cotton', 'Woody' . . . and so on. Indeed, few people ever did know that the real name of one of our most famous street characters — 'Weatherbird' — was actually Alfred Mills.

Street parades are perhaps the most overt and colourful expressions of traditions and neither Hamilton nor St George seem to neglect any opportunity to stage a rousing procession. Both of these towns, along with the Naval Dockyard in Somerset, have

Bermuda Day celebrations. (BERMUDA TOURISM)

been staging such events for several centuries. Ever since soldiers and sailors first began using Bermuda as a base, the byeways and highways have reverberated under the stomping of boots, the firing of salutes and the banging of drums. Today, this ongoing succession of military parades continues.

One of the most famous occurs each June, when Front Street becomes the picturesque setting for the **Queen's Birthday Parade**. This is a splendid example of Bermuda shining in all her finery for her most classical display of pomp and ceremony. The Governor arrives in a horse-drawn carriage, resplendent in white tropical uniform, bedecked with sword and medals, his head sporting a pith helmet with long flowing feathers cascading from its crown. The band of the Bermuda Regiment then leads a march-past which incorporates representatives from all local forces, including detachments from the Canadian, British and US bases in Bermuda. At Albouy's Point, a formation of artillery field guns duly booms an official salute to honour the Queen's birthday, after which the military parade marches off through the streets of Hamilton. The Governor then returns to Government House where he hosts an official birthday reception for several hundred local dignitaries and personally invited guests.

Two far more solemn parades are held towards the end of the year, when Bermuda pays her respects to her war dead. One is held in Hamilton on 11th November, and coincides with similar memorial services which are being conducted throughout the British Commonwealth on the same day. On the following Sunday, a second 'Service of Remembrance' is conducted at the East End, in St George. Both occasions involve marches by representatives from all the services, including the sea cadets, guides and scouts, and they are joined by Bermuda's own bemedalled war veterans. There

The Gombeys in procession. (BERMUDA TOURISM)

is always the customary two minutes' silence — a gesture of contemplative tribute to those who fell in battle — and then wreaths are laid at the base of the cenotaph. After a solitary bandsman has trumpetted 'The Last Post', the parade takes a final salute and marches away.

The band of the Bermuda Regiment is the inevitable focal point of all local military parades and is one of which Bermudians can be justifiably proud. Through its music, the band has helped to carry the islands' reputation and pride across the Caribbean, North America and Europe. Furthermore, the band's reputation is also reflected in its having been selected to lead the prestigious centuries-old 'Lord Mayor's Show' in London.

Of the band's numerous local public appearances, none is more fascinating than 'Beating the Retreat'. This is a very historic ceremony, stretching back hundreds of years into the era when individual regimental bands formally escorted their own soldiers from the field-of-battle, at the official end of each day's warring. Today, Bermuda regularly re-enacts this military ritual — with the Bermuda Regiment alternating with the kilted pipers and drummers of the Bermuda Cadet pipe band. Both Hamilton and St George host these impressive ceremonies and, in strict accordance with original practice, they are always held at dusk, throughout the year.

A couple of other similar events should also be mentioned. Each April, the 'Peppercorn Ceremony' is held in St George's. This event originated in 1816 and marks the occasion when the Freemasons of Lodge St George 266 pay their annual rent for the use of the historic State House. With the square invariably ringed with spectators and the Bermuda Regiment band playing appropriate music, Government representatives and members of the St George's Corporation watch the formally aproned Freemasons march in procession down from the State House and into King's Square. There, they publicly pay Bermuda's Governor the fee of one solitary peppercorn for the use of their premises for the coming year.

During October, at the other end of the island, the Dockyard hosts a similar traditional re-enactment called the 'Cannonball Ceremony'. This sees the formal presentation of a genuine, ancient cannonball to a representative of the Government — paid as the customary rent for the vast properties incorporated into the Maritime Museum. In the presence of many dignitaries, the Bermuda Regiment band and members of the public, a group of Sea Cadets solemnly carries into the keepyard a cedar bier on which is positioned the cannonball in question. Amidst drum rolls and flag-raising, the cannonball is then handed over to the Government, and the annual rent is thereby formally settled.

If ceremonious occasions epitomise a formal side to Bermudian culture, then the 'Bermuda Day Parade' shows Bermudians in one of their most relaxed moods. Always held on 24th May, this is the climax to the island-wide celebration of Heritage month and, for many Bermudians, is perhaps the most significant event on the year's social calendar. Originally, this festive occasion was known as 'Empire Day', the time once officially designated for the celebration of Queen Victoria's birthday. In practice, it

Overleaf: *Bermuda fitted dinghies racing in Hamilton harbour.* (BERMUDA TOURISM)

also became the day when locals took their first 'official' swim of the year; the day which specifically pinpointed the traditional start to another season of picnics, boating and beach-parties. Today, these latter traditions remain very much an integral part of the activities, but they are now heralded by what is surely the Island's most elaborate street parade.

The Bermuda Day parade starts early in the morning and the streets of Hamilton quickly begin bouncing with the magic of a carnival atmosphere. Groups of majorettes strut along the streets, twirling batons and stomping their feet to the beat of drums and the flurries of trumpets. Groups of dancers wearing bright and flamboyant costumes weave their way in and out of the colourful parade of floats, each sporting a generous sprinkling of local beauty queens who smile enchantingly and wave at the crowds along the route. Various bands play to the alternating rhythms of calypso, jazz and marching music as the parade gradually curls its way in pulsating splendour towards a public recreation field on the outskirts of the city. Here, after prominent speakers have lauded Bermuda's people and their rich heritage, the bands strike up once again and uninterrupted partying continues well into the night. The size and popularity of this parade have now helped to fill the lamented void left by the demise of one of its traditional forebears — the 'Floral Pageant', an Easter event which ironically grew to such remarkable and extravagant proportions that it outstripped the availability of local blooms.

Also on this same day of seemingly unbridled celebrations, St George's hosts another truly traditional activity — the annual sailboat races. This event has been held in the harbour for well over 150 years and is organised exclusively for the islands' own 'Bermuda fitted dinghy'. This sailboat is entirely unique to Bermuda and is clearly one which was evidently designed to carry the absolute maximum of sail, on the smallest possible low-swung hull. These unusual boats are remarkably fast and have been raced before crowds of cheering onlookers since the early nineteenth century. Vessels of all shapes and sizes congregate in the old town for this occasion, and the harbour is filled with rows of colourful flags and bunting, as festive crews of onlookers gather to watch the races.

Informality and spontaneity are the trademarks of many of the islands' traditions. Easter kite-flying, for example, is very much a family occasion when home-made kites take to the air from the early hours of the morning — and often remain aloft until darkness descends. Most Bermudians are taught the skills of kite-making as children and, even in this age of 'ready-mades', it is rewarding to find that the vast majority of Bermuda's kites continue to be hand-made — invariably in those selfsame six-sided or diamond designs used by their forebears. Many competitions are arranged throughout Bermuda for the largest, smallest and most traditional kites to fly success-fully through the air, whilst down at Horseshoe Bay hundreds of enthusiasts gather to enjoy a day of community kiting.

The truly traditional Bermuda kite should be made without resorting to nails or wire; the frames consist of thin stays of wood, each bound at the joints with twine. Sometimes a curved 'head' is incorporated by bending bamboo across the two leading arms. The panels of the completed frame are then carefully decorated with pieces of coloured tissue paper, so that each becomes an integral part of a mosaic design. Some kite-flyers fasten a string along the leading edge, which is then lined with narrow strips of paper. These are known as 'hummers' and account for the day-long noise which emanates from the skies during Easter. Kites are taken seriously here and Bermuda's very own 'Kite King Tuzo' actually gained international recognition both for himself and the island's kiting tradition by having a world kite-flying record acknowledged in the celebrated *Guinness Book of Records*.

Another traditional treat occurs on Boxing Day, the day after Christmas Day, when Bermuda's indigenous native dancers customarily take to the streets. They are called 'Gombeys', a word reputedly derived from a Bantu word meaning 'rhythm', and have an intriguing history which stems partly from Africa, partly from the West Indies and partly from the influences of North American Indians. Performing to the accompaniment of a rapid, rolling beat from several side-drums, the Gombeys do a type of dance which is decidedly acrobatic and certainly energetic. They carry tomahawks and bullwhips, incorporating them into the dance through mock threatening gestures which challenge fellow dancers on to steps which are ever more difficult. The Gombeys wear extremely colourful homemade costumes, with ornate capes decorated with mirrors and sequins draped across the shoulders; spectacular head-dresses crown their heads, with tall elegant peacock feathers swaying at the top. Each wears a mask to conceal his identity. By tradition, Gombeys have always been boys and men, although in recent years one or two girls have been noticed in some troupes. Gombey groups usually consist of a dozen or so dancers, with ages ranging from very young up to middle-age. As street performers, the Gombeys take a collection at the end of each performance. Although Boxing Day is their traditional time of the year, groups can

Cup Match, St George. (BERMUDA TOURISM)

be expected to make completely impromptu appearances anywhere, at anytime.

Traditions, of course, can be found in all areas of Bermudian life and are certainly too numerous to mention in their entirety. One of the most curious, however, is 'roof wetting'. Upon the completion of a building project — be it an office block or a private house — the owner, contractor, architect, and others who have contributed towards its construction, climb up on to the roof and officially conduct a brief service similar to a baptism. A bottle of black rum is broken open and its contents are poured over the newly completed roof. The tradition dates back several centuries and would appear to have connections with the practice of christening a newly laid boat.

Among sporting buffs, the traditional highlight of each year is 'Cup Match', a game of cricket which pits the most talented players from the East End of Bermuda, against the cricketing cream of the West End. This two-day cricket match is played at the start of August, at either Somerset or St George. It is of such great importance to most Bermudians that much of the island comes to a virtual halt for the duration of the game! The first ball is bowled at 10 a.m. and the last is received at approximately 6.30 p.m. Other than the tradional breaks for lunch and, yes, tea! this is a non-stop sporting festival. The stands are always packed to capacity, with many families opting to camp overnight in order to be assured of a seat on the following day. There is an unusual, almost carnival atmosphere to Cup Match, as people sing, dance, applaud, eat, keep score, shout encouragement to the cricketers, and even engage in 'Crown and Anchor' — the only occasion when Bermuda uses Nelson's blind eye to allow public gambling. In 1976, Cup Match celebrated its 75th anniversary. A set of four stamps was issued to mark the occasion.

On a lighter note, there are some traditions which are re-enacted solely for the

The Town Crier of St George with an errant visitor in the stocks!
(DAVID F. RAINE)

purpose of entertaining visitors. The best known of these is the regular 'Ducking' conducted by the Towne Crier of St George, during which one of the better known gossips of the town is fastened into the official ducking stool and dunked into the harbour several times, until she repents. (Tradition, of course, has always maintained that gossips were to be found among the womenfolk!) However, to be perfectly fair, drunkards were invariably found to be men, and so the Towne Crier usually manages to locate one miscreant, who is then unceremoniously bundled into the stocks and pelted with tomatoes. These re-enactments are usually performed in St George each Wednesday.

Finally, perhaps our most universally recognised traditional form of dress is that known as 'Bermuda shorts'. Indeed they are part of a formal dress-code. Bankers, teachers and businessmen wear them to work just as naturally as they wear white shirts, ties and blazers. Bermuda shorts are accepted for formal dining, including even the most prestigious of banquets, and seem not at all out of place under the flashing strobe lights of a night-club dance floor. Bermuda shorts are at least one tradition which we have quite willingly given to the world!

| 10 |
The Royal Naval Dockyard

Any mention of Bermuda's western-most tip automatically makes one think of the 'Dockyard'. This sprawling complex was once a key British naval base which completely dominated Ireland Island and generously spilt a variety of support-buildings on to adjacent Boaz and Watford Islands. Converted barrack blocks, unusual reinforced quaysides and terraced housing for bygone military families have survived as relics, visible indicators that the area beyond Somerset Village has indeed experienced a former life.

Today, the Dockyard accommodates Bermuda's **Maritime Museum**, an arts centre, the international **Marina Real Del Oeste** and innumerable small businesses ranging from boatyards through to a pottery and snack bars. But this is not the way things used to be; nor indeed is it the way things were meant to be according to the global defence plans which Britain once had for its mighty Empire.

Whereas the early Spanish and Portuguese sailors had tended to use Bermuda as little other than a mid-Atlantic signpost on their bullion runs back to Europe, it was the English who seemingly first realised that the true potential of these islands lay in their strategic location. When Admiral Somers and his shipwrecked party sat on the shoreline and looked out at the Atlantic Ocean stretching endlessly about them, horrendous notions that these were 'the Devil's Islands' must surely have been rapidly replaced by far more favourable reflections. These were no longer islands to be avoided and feared, or neglected because of an obvious lack of gold and silver, but were actually perfectly situated for observing the passing sea-borne traffic.

The British increasingly realised that from here they could sit, like wardens in a unique oceanic watchtower, recording the comings-and-goings of vessels of all nations. (In later years, Bermuda would be similarly used to track submarines, aircraft and rocket ships.) Perched atop Bermuda, Britannia would unquestionably and forever rule the waves. In order to protect this newly-acquired territory, the first settlers were instructed to build forts at all points around the islands. Meanwhile, politicians and military men carefully spent nearly two centuries contemplating how best this strategic advantage might be most effectively exploited.

The building of the Royal Naval Dockyard did not finally get underway until Ireland Island was bought by the British Government in 1809, although some preliminary surveying had commenced two years earlier under the supervision of Vice-Admiral Sir John Warren. The basic plan was to construct a facility which could be used as a well-fortified centre for repairing and supplying the fleet in this section of the Atlantic. From here too, the naval heirarchy envisaged being able to keep a handy yet distant eye on the protection of British interests and possessions in North America and the Caribbean.

Twin clock towers in the Naval Dockyard. (MICHAEL BOURNE)

Looking at these thick nineteenth century walls, it is easy to understand why the Victorians were confident that the British Empire could never collapse. Indeed the original builders made the walls of the victualling yard so deep that they comfortably contained water-tanks, coal storage chambers and a cooperage. Construction was not finally regarded as complete until about 1897 when Vice-Admiral Sir John Fisher finalised some smaller lingering projects and generally cleared out the debris of several decades of construction.

Much of the workforce for this venture was provided in the form of convict labour dispatched from England. It was a curious conglomeration of debtors, petty thieves, Irish rebels, convicted poachers, unemployed mill-workers and gentlemen of undesirable political persuasions. The first group arrived in 1824 and by the time that the last batch were repatriated in 1862, over 2000 of them had been laid to rest in Bermuda, in unmarked graves. The convicts were housed in hulks anchored near Grassy Bay. There, in disused men-of-war hulls converted to provide spartan sleeping and eating quarters below deck, these miserable wretches served out their sentences. Conditions were harsh and the work was hard; sympathy was non-existent. In 1859, a riot broke out on board the hulk *Medway* between Irish and English nationalists; the wardens reacted by closing the hatches and simply leaving them to it. Scores of convicts were injured during the ensuing mêlée in the darkness below; one was killed.

When the United States declared war on Britain in 1812, Bermuda's role suddenly became vital as a staging post for the Royal Navy. Blockades were orchestrated from

Overleaf: *Aerial view of the Royal Naval Dockyard showing the Maritime Museum in the foreground.* (THE BERMUDA MARITIME MUSEUM)

here and it was from these waters that the fleet departed in 1814 for Chesapeake Bay, which resulted in the infamous burning of Washington by the victorious British. Indeed, the Admiral of that fleet, Sir George Cockburn, felt so indebted to the pilot who had initially guided the main convoy safely through the reefs at the very start of the campaign that he presented an inscribed brooch to the good man's wife, as a gesture of personal gratitude.

The war of 1812 also incidentally provided the Dockyard with an additional source of labour. With the arrival of so many British vessels in American waters, hundreds of slaves sought refuge on their decks. Many of them were subsequently brought to Bermuda where they were employed as free wage-earners at the Dockyard. By 1823, excluding convicts, the complex engaged a regular staff of 74 Englishmen, 54 locals, 164 paid labourers and 45 others,including pilots. Together they built storehouses for ammunition, foodstuffs and servicing equipment; there was a hospital, a cemetery, a church and a large barracks designed to accommodate 400 of the élite Royal Marines. (This latter structure was eventually converted into Bermuda's main prison, 'Casemates'.)

From meagre wooden stockade beginnings the Dockyard soon expanded into fortress proportions. The entire area was encircled by castle-like walls and around one section there was even a moat. The main entrances were huge gateways, which seemed only to lack portcullises and battlements for pouring hot oil over! Certain that the development had somehow got out of hand, in 1848 a somewhat bewildered and bemused Lord Dundonald felt obliged to describe it as a wonder of error. 'There is nothing to defend!' he bellowed at the echoing walls. 'Inside is a void!' To some extent, of course, he was correct.

Although the Dockyard's prime function was to service vessels of the Royal Navy, and its allies, it soon became far more than just a military installation. Local apprentices were taken on at the age of thirteen and were taught a trade for the next six or so years before qualifying; there was a ginger beer factory operating here from 1860 right up until 1944. The Spar Yard was often used as a theatre and the Commissioner's House, overlooking the entire development, was the site of many grand balls and banquets. From 1830 to 1850, the resident victualling agent, Mr Samuel Truscott, kindly organised boating regattas for British officers and Bermudians alike; there were dances, parties and marriages. The Dockyard staffed its own forge; there was a resident blacksmith; the workers made buoys to mark the complicated channels, whilst others cast tombstones to mark where the unfortunate fell. But above all else, there were shipyards.

Between 1795 and 1840, Bermuda built a variety of fifty schooners and sloops for the Royal Navy, each based upon plans provided by the Admiralty. This was also the place where repairs were carried out on vessels damaged in skirmishes with enemy boats. It was from here that English privateers — truly little more than authorised pirates — scoured the seas looking for prizes to engage and capture. Countless were towed into Bermuda and many captured cargoes were auctioned in the local market. By the end of the nineteenth century, Bermuda's Dockyard had firmly established itself as 'the Gibraltar of the West'.

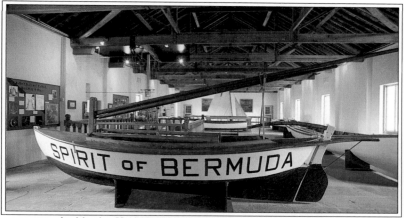

Inside the Maritime Museum. (BERMUDA MARITIME MUSEUM)

Today, the Royal Navy maintains only a small military presence on Ireland Island. However, it still remains the strategic centre for fleets patrolling the Atlantic and Caribbean Basin; NATO vessels are also frequent visitors to these waters. In 1939 the HMS *Ajax* and HMS *Exeter* came here for additional supplies during the course of their legendary chase of the German battleship *Admiral Graf Spee*. More recently, ships returning from the Falklands War paused here on their way back home. The Dockyard's function remains what it has always been: to refuel and service British and other ships passing through the area.

Most of the Dockyard buildings have now assumed other purposes. By far the most impressive is that grouping which constitutes the Maritime Museum. Opened on 17th February, 1975 by Her Majesty the Queen, this has rapidly developed into the country's prime depository of artefacts, records and treasures relating to Bermuda's maritime history. Here the serious researcher and casual visitor alike can find displays of models, maps and memorabilia spanning centuries of developments and contributions which the Dockyard has made; there are exhibits of treasures recovered from galleons which sank off the reefs long before man ever set his foot on these shores. As the need arises, other areas and buildings are drawn into use. The Earl Mountbatten of Burma opened the **Keepyard Park** in 1975; Princess Margaret opened the **Forster Cooper Building** in 1984.

The old **Cooperage**, firmly nestled into the walls of the victualling yard, has become a craft centre where a variety of locally-made products are demonstrated and sold. Nearby, the **Dockyard Arts Centre** has become the home of an art gallery, in which local and visiting artists exhibit their work. The bay in which the convict hulks once lay has been converted into a modern international marina. Large cruise-ships dock alongside its enclosing walls.

In many respects, however, the modern-day Dockyard has become simply an updated version of what it has always been — a key operational and social focal point at Bermuda's western-most tip.

| 11 |
A touch of culinary flavour

We should always be somewhat sceptical when reading that one dish or another is absolutely typical of any country. It is neither easy nor particularly accurate to announce unequivocably that the majority favours one food or another above all others. This type of generalisation leads to the same misleading stereotyping which would have us believe that Americans eat nothing other than hamburgers, or that the British continuously top themselves up with fish-and-chips.

However, having said that, anyone genuinely curious to know which foods Bermudians themselves regard as being truly typical would probably find the best answers laid out on the counter at a local social function such as a school or church 'potluck supper'. It is here that families cater directly for the palates of each other, cooking speciality dishes solely for the culinary pleasure of one another. On such occasions, the observer will find an abundance of salads and coleslaws; trays of macaroni-and-cheese wedged between platters of chicken and fried fish, banana bread and carrot cakes. Soups will doubtless be either fish chowder, or red-bean soup generously laced with Portuguese chirico sausage. Over on the sales table, there will be jams and chutneys made from loquats, bay grapes, Surinam cherries, oranges and lemons.

The more discerning eye may also perhaps notice bowls of a very popular rice dish known as 'Hopping John', or more simply as 'Peas'n rice'. For many Bermudians, this is virtually a staple feature of their diet. It originates from the West Indies and a lot of friendly rivalry still exists among the islands' home cooks, who argue that only those with a direct line of descent back into the Caribbean can really make 'Peas'n rice' properly. Whoever 'John' was, or indeed why he was 'hopping', we will surely never know.

Essentially, 'Hopping John' consists of black-eyed peas boiled with rice. The art to its preparation appears to lie in successfully cooking the ingredients in tandem, whilst simultaneously preventing the rice from becoming sticky and the peas too squashy — evidently not as easy as it seems. The preferred seasonings which get added into the pot are almost as numerous as the chefs themselves. Some use a few pinches of parsley and thyme, others add rosemary, or tarragon, or basil. There are others who think that the finished dish is incomplete without finely-diced chicken or ham. Whichever, it is prepared to personal tastes and is an inexpensive family meal — similar in that respect to Moroccan cous-cous.

Another interesting place to catch a glimpse of the authentic Bermudian diet is through the serving-hatch of one of the many Government certified lunch wagons. Here it will be quickly noted that beef and mussel pies far outnumber lunchtime requests for hot-dogs; that hamburgers are always homemade from a jealously-

Hogfish supper (DEPARTMENT OF TOURISM, BERMUDA)

guarded family recipe and that fish cakes are in constant demand.

Fish cakes are a very popular and nutritious food. Ask Mrs Winifred Sewell of St George's how she makes hers and without hesitation this generous lady will open the unwritten recipe book in her memory and freely rattle off the details. She uses salted codfish and leaves it to soak overnight. The brine is then drained away and fresh water is poured into the pan alongside peeled potatoes. Together they are boiled for slightly less than an hour. She invariably sprinkles a little parsley, a few peppers and thyme into the water, as well as adding chopped onion for extra flavour.

Once the fish and potatoes are cooked, the water is drained off and the fish and potatoes are thoroughly mashed. Just before frying, she blends an egg or two into the mixture. The eggs help to bind the fish cakes together; however, she hastily points out that if they are added too early during the preparation there is a tendency for the finished products to be too watery. She heats vegetable fat in a pan and, using a tablespoon as a measuring scoop, she rolls the cakes into shape by hand. They are covered with a fine coating of flour to give them a thin crust, and then fried. She estimates that one pound of codfish and six medium potatoes will make two dozen fish cakes.

Like most other islanders, Bermudians eat fish as often as possible. They eat it boiled, fried in batter, marinated in vinegar. They barbecue wahoo and tuna steaks, and pop jacks into shallow pans and cook them whole. They bake hind, hogfish and bonito.They also make some of the finest chowders that can be found anywhere.

For the unacquainted, chowder is a fish soup, made quite basically by boiling the head and leftovers of a fish for a long period of time, so as to elicit all of the inherent and natural goodness from the carcass. During the brewing the cook adds various herbs and spices. Some chefs include onions and tomatoes; other frown at these and include potatoes and diced green peppers. Clearly, it is all very much a matter of flavouring to personal taste.

However, the key to any successful chowder unquestionably lies in the time allotted to the simmering of the brew. Here, at least, there is widespread belief common among chowder makers that the longer it is allowed to simmer, the better it will taste. I still have the most vivid recollection of standing on a beach at the back of St David's Island, some years back, and talking to the late 'Bumpy' Pitcher whilst he was cooking chowder in a very large black pot. He had had this particular cauldron of chowder on the go for three days, carefully simmering over a driftwood fire which he had built on the seashore. This was truly idyllic outdoor cooking — the wood crackling and a pot simmering to the gentle roll of waves breaking on to the sands. He reckoned that it would be fine and ripe in another couple of days! Sure enough, we met up again at the appointed hour and he dug a ladle into the pot and scooped up one of the finest chowders ever made. With the truest capacity of character and stomach he poured black rum into the chowder before lifting a spoon; others opt for sherry peppers. Either way, no self-respecting Bermudian would dream of taking chowder without one or the other of these final ingredients, or both. (Bumpy's son Bernell apparently inherited some of this talent, for he is now the resident chef at the widely respected 'Black Horse Tavern', on St David's Island.)

To experience one of the most traditional Bermudian meals, one has to appreciate that for many the culinary climax to the entire week is actually Sunday breakfast, and a hearty helping of 'Codfish and bananas'. The precise origins of this distinctive kitchen delight are not only blurred, but are also not particularly important to the palate. Bermudians have certainly been eating salted codfish since the early seventeenth century when, in those distant days before refrigeration, it was realised that only barrels of salted fish could be safely preserved for human consumption in this humid sub-tropical climate. Then, as now, most of it was imported from the Maritime Provinces of Canada and perhaps somewhere over there lie the roots of what has evolved into this unusual meal. It is certainly so deeply entrenched as a weekly table platter that no reputable café would even bother to open on a Sunday morning if 'Codfish and bananas' was not at the top of their breakfast menu. Sporting groups often organise 'Codfish and bananas' as a certain means of quickly raising funds.

The dish is prepared from boneless, salted codfish, which has been washed and then soaked for two to three hours to remove some of the saltiness of the brine. Because the fish portions are quite thick, it is then left to soak overnight in another pan of water. In many households, for some reason or the other, the designated cook for this particular dish is frequently the man. Indeed, it was once my pleasure, after an all-night gathering, to watch the pre-dawn skies unfolding their colours through the kitchen window at the home of 'Black Wolf' Fox as he, like many others that day, started to make Sunday breakfast.

He began the ritual by draining the overnight water away and then gently boiling the fish in fresh water for about an hour. In the same pot he also placed whole, peeled potatoes which were therefore cooking at the same time as the fish. It was then lightly seasoned with a few pinches of this and a few pinches of that, each added beyond my scrutiny, but obviously to a customary and familiar recipe. Whilst all of this was quietly bubbling in the pot, the chef was busy cutting several bananas into slices. By preference they were true Bermudian bananas, picked from the back garden, although some families prefer the sweeter 'strawberry' bananas sometimes known as plantains. These were laid on a side dish. Most Bermudians, however, prefer to put the slices of banana on top of the potatoes and eat it all together. By seven thirty, the meal was all over; we had finished every last scrap and were clearing the table and washing the dishes. The whole day and another week lay ahead and we felt well-satisfied and well-equipped to face it. A one pound packet of fish and four to six medium-sized potatoes provide enough food for about three people. As the sun came up, so Black Wolf's 'Codfish and bananas' went down.

Incidentally, 'Codfish and bananas' is often eaten with some simple sauces poured over the top. One of these consists of hard-boiled egg, chopped-up and then mixed with melted butter and a little parsley. I remember one cook down at Harris Bay who finely diced some onion, fried it with browned bacon, and then used that as a topping, mixed with butter.

At Christmas time, no Bermudian table is complete without its 'Cassava pie'. Of all the local foods, this is probably among the most traditional. Cassava is a root-crop which grows to about six feet in height. In days of yore, children were set the task of pulling the plants and cutting off the root. Their next job was to peel the root itself and then laboriously grate the meat until it was all finely shredded. This pulp was then wrapped into a piece of muslin and hung outside for the night, so that the liquid could drain free. There was a staunchly held belief that if ingested, the watery substance in the cassava was potentially a fatal poison; however, we now know that, rather than containing poison, it was the high level of starch which had so frequently induced stomach pains and vomiting. (Some wives left the liquid residue out in the sun to evaporate — and used the starch itself in other domestic chores.)

Today, almost no one ever has to confront the exhausting preparation of raw cassava, although there are indeed still some stalwarts who continue to prepare it in this tedious but traditional manner. It can instead be bought already prepared from most stores. Five pounds of cassava, mixed with a dozen eggs and one pound of butter, will make an ample quantity of food for a family.

These main ingredients have to be fully blended into a sponge-like pastry and, according to one respected cook from Slip Road, off Mullet Bay, nutmeg can also be sprinkled into it along with some salt and two cups of sugar. The quantities of each of these, of course, will vary according to taste. Whilst this is being prepared, a two pound box of chicken should be cooked by boiling. When that is ready, it has to be totally deboned and the meat then cut into small pieces. Part of the cassava mixture is then used as a liner for the base of a pre-greased and floured dish; this will be the bottom of the pie. Next the chicken is added and a layer of cassava is laid over the top. The dish is then placed into an oven at 350° F and cooked for about two-and-a-half hours. To all Bermudians, this culinary speciality is just as essential to the Christmas table as is the turkey and its trimmings.

Traditional Bermudian breakfast: Codfish and bananas.
(DEPARTMENT OF TOURISM, BERMUDA)

Naturally, there are innumerable other dishes which Bermudians regularly enjoy, whether eaten at home or in a restaurant. Shark is quite popular, as are mussel pies, conch stew and various mildly-curried platters. Although shark can be conveniently cut into steaks and either fried or barbecued, it is more commonly eaten when blended with various herbs and served as an entrée, often on 'fingers' of toast. Shark meat is to be treated with considerable caution, however, and no chef will begin to prepare 'shark hash' until the colour of the liver has been verified. If it is whitish, it can be used — any other colour and the entire fish is deemed to be unhealthy, and is discarded. One incidental by-product of the shark is its oil. When drained from the liver it can be sealed inside a bottle and left outside to become a very effective barometer. Old-timers continue to shun contemporary meteorological sciences and rely completely upon their shark oil for predicting storms.

In eating preferences, Bermudians generally tend to shun packaged mixes and favour genuine home-baked goods. Many local corner stores sell limited supplies of beef pies during lunchtime, made by someone in the neighbourhood. Sales are always brisk and 'Johnny-come-lately' gets none!

For those with a true yearning for culinary adventure, perhaps the most remarkable selection of unusual seafoods in Bermuda is to be found at 'Dennis's Hideaway', on the eastern tip of St David's Island. Here, in his own kitchen, Dennis Lamb and his son Graham prepare conch fritters, conch stew, shark hash, fish chowder, mussels and fried fish — even a turtle steak has been known to be served when available. Nearby, also on St David's Island, 'The Black Horse Tavern' is a very popular eatery for locals in search of fish and fine homemade chowders and stews. 'Clyde's Cafe', over in St George's, is another spot frequented by Bermudians wanting fish dishes and a good good chowder. In Somerset, 'Woody's' also offers an outstanding array of fish and various local plates. Of course, if you don't have time to stop and sit for a meal, Degraff's lunch wagon in Hamilton City Hall carpark serves excellent home-made pies and hamburgers.

Wherever the newcomer to these islands cares to venture, the quest for the authentic Bermudian cuisine can be made with absolute confidence, thanks to a succession of health regulations which the Bermudian Government stringently enforces on all types of kitchens and eating places, both large and small.

| 12 |
Some medicinal folklore

It is an old adage that man usually only starts to apply his initiative when he finds himself stranded and stripped of all of the customary conveniences. Only then does he begin to appreciate what Nature has provided, and start to exploit what lies at hand. It's a truism that has held firmly throughout history and legend, from Robinson Crusoe through to Davy Crockett, and certainly for shipwrecked survivors of the *Sea Venture*.

Many of the earliest uses to which Bermuda's forebears put nature have inevitably become redundant over the centuries. The first Bermudians, for example, soon found that the prickly pear and other berries were ideal for the making of fabric dyes. It is difficult now to locate any living soul who can recall having used them for that purpose, other than Bermudian weaver Gwen Cann who often resorts to natural dyes. Similarly, I doubt that any of us would trust our contemporaries to manipulate the brew of berries from the palmetto, and make the highly potent beverage once known as 'Bibby' — a drink so strong that efforts to ban its open manufacture date back to 1661!

It is inevitable that some of the original uses of our natural resources have simply faded into perpetual oblivion, along with other unrecorded memories of our ancestors; others have become suffocated beneath layers of archival dust. Others still have become so elaborately embroidered that it is difficult to pick out the threads of truth: thay have become distorted, with fact and fiction so bewilderingly blended into a single reality that we may never unravel the original twine. This is particularly so in the realm of natural cures and remedies which may or may not have been used in the past. One can still hear wise men talking about cobwebs being neatly folded into pads which, when applied to a swelling, helped it to go down. Others speak with straight, expressionless faces of live cockroaches being rather bizarrely swallowed in order to clear a sore throat. Only the glint of an eye betrays the inherent doubts of the story-teller.

Not all of the natural cures and treatments, however, are impossible to identify. Many were used in Bermuda and there is ample evidence to testify to their varying levels of success; some are probably still randomly used today. There must be many grandparents who can take children by the hand and give them a guided medicinal tour of the garden. Christie Smith, a highly respected fisherman from Tucker's Town, once took me for a stroll over a small piece of rough land and within a few minutes he had identified close to twenty different weeds and grasses, and told me their curative properties. As an aside, he outlined the method for using a centipede to make an antidote for serious insect bites, including its own!

Of course, in reality one only has to leap back through a generation or two in order to find living people who were raised during those times when many tonics and ointments were homemade, using the leaves from plants in the backyard. The fact that their only yardstick for success was that it seemed to work neither invalidates their expertise nor does it diminish the validity of their concoctions. Without scientific know-how, they made their environment work for them. They saved some lives, healed cuts, cured fevers and mended injuries.

A quiet chat with the late Mrs Lilian Lambe of St George's was always a fine way to gain a true insight into those forgotten ways. She would fondly remember those days and generously talk about the times long before the old town ever had regular doctors; when trips to Hamilton were an extraordinary adventure not experienced by everyone; when mothers had to act swiftly and assuredly to tend to the daily problems of child-rearing. Of all the potential illnesses which regularly faced Bermudians at the beginning of this century, coughs, colds and fevers were among Mrs Lambe's prime concerns. That she survived childhood, raised a family and became a great-grandmother is testimony in itself to the success of this gentle lady's knowledge in such matters. She was far from being exceptionally gifted or unique, it was simply that herbal medicine was as natural to her and her neighbours as computer technology is to Bermudian school children today.

One conventional cure for coughs required the making of a simple syrup. Cedar berries were most commonly used. They were collected along the wayside and put into a pot. Together with several generous cupfuls of plain sugar, the berries were boiled in water for many hours until much of the liquid had evaporated and the residue had assumed the consistency of a syrup. Taken by the spoonful every few hours, it was sure to relieve the most common coughs.

Cedar berries. (DR. ROBERTA DOW)

Match-me-if-you-can plant. (DR. ROBERTA DOW)

Colds were some of the perennial ailments confronting Bermudians, just as they do today. There were two very popular remedies for this problem. The first involved the use of small white Bermuda onions. These were cut into very small pieces and then placed into an airtight jar, with a couple of scoops of brown sugar. This was then placed out in the sun and left to cure all on its own, for a week or so. The juices from the onions eventually merged with the sugar and created a syrup with the correct properties to cure the common cold. Lemon-grass tea was another favourite, made from a broad-leafed grass. The leaves and stalks were boiled with sugar and, sometimes, a squirt or two of juice from a real lemon was added. Many mothers also took a small quantity of the commercially produced 'Vicks Vapour Rub' and melted that into the brew, as a bonus. When drunk, there was every confidence that the cold would be gone in a day or two.

Beverages and linctuses, of course, were not the only remedies which these early herbalists used to produce. Ointments and poultices were also an essential part of their armoury in the fight against injury and sickness. Of all of the plants growing in Bermuda, the 'match-me-if-you-can' was the most important for curing fevers; in fact, it was so highly regarded for its natural properties that many youngsters grew up knowing it only by the name 'life leaf'. The leaves were gathered and mashed into a firm pulp which, just like a pastry, could then be rolled flat and shaped to convenience. It was then placed on both wrists as well as the forehead, and held in place by a handkerchief which had previously been soaked in pure alcohol. Some claim that the fever began to go down straightaway; on occasion it was found necessary to repeat the performance once more after a couple of hours, using fresh leaves.

Cuts and sprains could be effectively treated with an ointment made from the elderberry bush. Petals were taken from the flowers and boiled in water, with a scoop of cooking lard. When allowed to harden, the resulting ointment was a proven antiseptic cream used to treat most minor cuts and injuries, and was also effective in relieving sprains and bruises. I have spoken to one lady who sports a substantial scar on her wrist, caused by accidentally pushing her hand through a piece of glass when she was a child. The prolific bleeding was brought under control by applying a tourniquet — but the congealing of the blood at the entrance to the deep wound was apparently accomplished by a relative crushing some wild parsley with the leaves from a weed, and fastening that over the injury. The weed was that known in the vernacular as 'plantain grass' — a broad-leafed plant still found in lawns and verges, distinctive in appearance for the tall stem which rises from its centre like a miniature bullrush. The application had obviously worked; the evidence was before my eyes.

General aches and pains were treated by another concoction. Parents would gather some wood shavings from pitch pine and place them in a storage jar, liberally soaked in black rum. This was then left out in the sun for a few days to cure. The liquid was then drained away and used to help in treating ailments such as rheumatism, strained muscles and similar bodily aches and pains. Along with cedar, pitch pine was a wood widely used here in construction, and is particularly noteworthy in that it 'bleeds' more sap than cedar.

Among the more intriguing of these old remedies, and perhaps most understandable today, involved the use of a liquid derived from poppies, to ease teething problems among babies. The petals were removed from flowering poppies and placed in a jar with brown sugar; the good Mrs Lambe also conceded that sometimes the seeds were put into the jar as well. This was then placed out into the sun and allowed to cure under its natural heat for several days. The residue was then drained out and kept

'Lemon grass'. (DR. ROBERTA DOW)

in a bottle. When rubbed over the gums, its soothing action was almost instantaneous. Evidently, most houses kept a small stock of this soothing tonic — it certainly assured a peaceful neighbourhood! — and the older children were forbidden to sneak a spoonful, because it tended to make them drowsy. Elsewhere in the world, of course, other communities had also recognised the soothing properties of the poppy, without the medical background to identify its beneficial derivative, morphine.

Without doubt, Bermudians survived on these and other remedies for three centuries; they experimented with the natural world around them and adapted the plant-life to cure their many ills.

| 13 |
A haven for artists

As if they were irresistible magnets, Bermuda's natural beauty and serene atmosphere have traditionally lured writers, painters and composers towards her shores.

Poet Tom Moore was here in 1804, ostensibly as Registrar to the Admiralty Court, and spent many months in the grounds of the Walsingham property penning prose to 'Nea', a young lady from St George's. Over two hundred years earlier, English poet John Donne had sailed through these waters and composed 'The Calm' and 'The Storm'. American writer Mark Twain was a frequent visitor to Bermuda during the last twenty or so years of his life; it was he who reputedly sat in a rocking-chair overlooking Hamilton Harbour and graciously pronounced that whilst others might choose to visit Paradise, he would prefer to remain in Bermuda. At the same time, in the nearby Hamilton Princess Hotel, writer Rudyard Kipling frequently gave public readings to Bermudians from *The Jungle Book*.

British dramatist Sir Terrence Rattigan wrote many of his plays at his home overlooking the South Shore in Smith's Parish. The famous lyricist Noel Coward composed a great number of his tunes at 'Spithead', a house which he once owned along the Harbour Road. Interestingly enough, the American playwright Eugene O'Neill also owned the same estate at one time and his daughter Oona was born in Bermuda, in 1925. At the tender age of eighteen, she became wife of entertainer Charlie Chaplin, and thus that celebrated family also spent much time vacationing from the house. Canadian novelist Edwin Leather not only lives here, but also enjoys the distinction of having once served a term as Bermuda's Governor.

British composer the late Geoffrey Tankard was a long-time resident, finding in Bermuda the correct ambience for arranging music and preparing for his recitals. More recently, John Lennon sought refuge in Bermuda to compose most of the tunes for what became his last recordings. He spent much time strolling through the Botanical Gardens, named the album 'Double Fantasy' after an orchid which he saw there, and wrote the music at a house in Fairylands, which he rented for the summer months prior to his death.

American watercolourist Winslow Homer came here several times in the period 1899 to 1900, and painted some of his finest works in and around the Salt Kettle area. Ever since Homer visited Bermuda there has been a continuous parade of recognised artists coming from all over the world to paint the island's beauty and elegance. As a result, 'The Masterworks Foundation' was formed during the 1980s in order to try to repatriate as many as possible of the paintings done by these earlier

Overleaf: *Spithead, whose owners have included Noel Coward and Eugene O'Neill.*(DEPARTMENT OF TOURISM, BERMUDA)

distinguished visitors. These can now be seen at a continuous exhibition in the gallery on Front Street in Hamilton.

Bermuda, of course, has also produced her own roster of internationally respected artisans.

Sisters Ethel and Catherine Tucker captured the essence of Bermuda's personality in the era prior to the advent of motor vehicles (1947) and found their paintings highly-prized by not only local collectors but by dealers from all over North America and Europe. At the same time, May Middleton was quietly producing watercolours of Bermuda's plants and flowers which were not only destined to grace houses at home and overseas, but also brought her subsequent fame as an illustrator of floral books.

Perhaps the most beloved of Bermudian painters was Charles Lloyd Tucker, whose legacy includes sculptures, canvases in the post-Impressionistic style and a multitude of watercolour paintings. Born in 1913, he graduated through the local school system and then went to England to study music, with the hope of eventually becoming a concert pianist. Instead, he found himself increasingly more interested in courses focusing on art, architecture and design, and he gradually developed a feeling for oils and watercolours as his preferred media. During the 1950s his work was shown throughout Europe and was also included in exhibits which toured Africa, Australia, North America and Britain. In the 1960s, he held one-man shows in Bermuda, was featured in displays in the West Indies and the United States, and somehow still managed to play the church organ and teach at school. He passed away quite unexpectedly in 1971, long before reaching the true peak of his talents.

Among today's painters, Alfred Birdsey is unquestionably the most celebrated; arguably, he might even by the most internationally-respected Bermudian artist of all time. He was actually born in England, in 1912, but has lived in Bermuda since he was seven years old. As a young man he worked with an architect from Philadelphia, but his paintings owe less to this exposure than they do to his association with the American painter Joe Jones. Through Jones, Birdsey developed his own appreciation for the oriental concepts of space, abstraction and simplification — ingredients which have evolved into his own, universally recognisable, style. For the last thirty years, his works have been collected and shown all over the world. Alfred Birdsey also has two highly talented daughters: Joanne Birdsey Linberg and Antoinette Davis. Each enjoys an independent reputation as a watercolourist.

The post-war period has produced many artists of stature: Joy Bluck Waters, Hereward Watlington and Mary Zuill have all acquired international recognition. Like Birdsey, Mary Zuill maintains a working studio which is open to the public; both studios are just outside Hamilton, in Paget Parish.

Among the most active of Bermuda's contemporary professional artists, particular reference should also be made to the following:

Joan Forbes   Educated both at home and overseas, Joan's empathy with her native island is reflected in her paintings of Bermudian scenes and flowers. Many of her originals have been made into prints. Her work has been regularly exhibited in major shows in Bermuda and is frequently displayed throughout Canada. She operates her own gallery, 'Art House', in Paget.

'East Broadway, Hamilton' — a painting by Christopher Grimes.
(DAVID F. RAINE)

Eldon Trimingham   A professional painter and avid sailor since childhood, Eldon is Bermuda's major marine artist. His work is internationally respected for its meticulously researched accuracy and hangs in various museums and private collections. He is a member of the prestigious American Society of Marine Artists.

Desmond Fountain   The distinguished graduate of several leading art colleges in England, Desmond is Bermuda's most famous sculptor. He had held numerous local exhibitions, and his bronze figures have also been shown at some of the most prestigious galleries in London and New York. Among his larger works is the outstanding statue of Sir George Somers, in St George's. The subject of several published articles, he is the first Bermudian ever to be elected as a Fellow of the Royal Society of British Sculptors.

Mary Powell   Mary's Bermudian views and sea-scapes have long been part of both private and public collections at home and overseas. Developing a talent which she fostered as a child, Mary is a very active and experimental painter who has studied under American watercolourist Carl Schumltz and still travels to workshops abroad.

Christopher Grimes   A graduate of the Bermuda Technical Institute, Christopher has devoted much of his artistic career to studying old photographs and documents, acquiring information which he then uses meticulously to reconstruct the unique scenes of Bermuda in years gone by. His paintings are invariably done in oil and have been bought by collectors both in Bermuda and overseas. He works primarily through commissions, from his studio in Southampton.

'Ivy Cottage' — a painting by Mary Powell. (DAVID F. RAINE)

Jill Amos Raine   Born in England, Jill has lived in Bermuda since childhood. She enjoys a joint reputation as the island's leading enamellist and as one of its prominent watercolourists. Her work has been included in many overseas craft displays as part of Bermuda Government promotions. In 1976, she represented the island at the Caribbean Arts Festival in Jamaica. Invited to do the painting for the offical print used to celebrate Bermuda's 375th Anniversary, subsequent limited edition prints of her. paintings have rapidly become very collectable.

Chesley Trott   Throughout the islands' history, there can have been very few wood-sculptors who have ever had such a sensitive understanding for Bermuda's native cedar. Using unrivalled skill and patience, Chesley channels his creativity through a filter which is partly traditional Africa and partly modernist Henry Moore. The result is a unique blend of carving which has been frequently exhibited locally and is included in collections throughout the world. He teaches art, and works at his private studio in Southampton.

Diana Amos   Born in Bermuda, Diana studied art in England and then returned home as an art lecturer at the Bermuda College. Working in both oils and watercolour, she has acquired considerable respect for accurately capturing the natural hues and true character of her island home. She has successfully exhibited in Bermuda, Britain, USA and Jamaica. Her husband is Eric Amos, a wildlife artist particularly well-known for his paintings of birds in their natural settings. She exhibits at 'The Windjammer Gallery'.

Kath Bell   Bermuda's leading dollmaker, Kath returned to Bermuda after studying in Britain and devoted her career to using her craft as a vehicle for immortalising the country's past and present personalities. Particularly well-known for the accuracy with which she researches the costumes of her historical figures, she has also made doll-portraits of many of Bermuda's leading political figures. She has a private studio in Paget and exhibits exclusively at 'The Bridge House Art Gallery' in St George's.

In addition to private ventures, there are two other major bodies which help in the encouragement and development of the arts in Bermuda. By far the most visible of these is the **Bermuda Society of Arts**, an independent organisation which is managed by its own membership of practising local artists. In addition to having a constantly changing series of exhibitions in the exhibition gallery at the **City Hall**, in Hamilton, the BSA is also very active in organising lectures and slide shows. Over the years, an increasingly significant aspect of the Society's activities has been the arrangement of workshops and demonstrations for its membership — directed not only by distinguished residents but also by leading artists brought in from overseas. Included on the list of those who have addressed the Society over the years are famed British portrait painters Sam Morse-Brown and Tony Harper; American watercolourists Carl Schmultz and Jim Scott, and English artists Tom Coates and Bill Pickering.

The **Bermuda Arts Council** serves as a quasi-Government body, specifically committed to encouraging all aspects of the arts in Bermuda. Its members are officially appointed. In addition to serving as a wide-ranging think-tank for related ideas, the appointees assume an advisory function to the general public as a whole. Their diverse interests embrace the performing arts from dance to drama, photography, cultural displays, literature, film and so on. The Arts Council is the main focal-point for consultations on all topics relating to Bermuda's rich and varied cultural heritage.

Overleaf: *Horseshoe Bay.* (G.W. LENNOX)

|14|
Places to go, people to see...

People who visit these islands, as well as those of us who live here, never cease to marvel at the great variety of things that there are to do. Bermuda may indeed be very small, but no matter what different interests and tastes each individual may have, there really is something for everyone, on land or sea.

Bermuda is a natural centre for anyone with even the most casual interest in the sea. Even those who reap no satisfaction whatsoever from sunbathing on a beach can find plenty of other distractions nearby. It can be quite mesmerising, for example, to stand beneath the cliffs and see longtails circling gracefully overhead; or to watch their gently flapped restraints as they approach the nesting ledges. It is restful merely to sit on the rocks and watch the waves breaking on the reefs, so clearly visible everywhere along the **South Shore**. Ruddy turnstones, sandpipers and golden plovers are usually pecking their way up and down the beaches looking for shrimps and other things to eat amidst the bubbles, leaves and stems of the ubiquitous sargasso weed.

You don't need to amble far along the rocks before finding countless crabs, anemones and fishes to watch. There are molluscs galore, with everything represented from oysters, clams and barnacles, through to a miscellany of periwinkles. Chitons and other crustaceans abound in rock pools whilst tiny inlets yield an unending variety of smaller fish to create an entirely natural aquarium. Among the more common fishes to be seen are sergeant majors, snappers, squirrelfish, wrasse, blue tangos and angelfish; whilst out in the deeper swells the vegetarian parrotfish peck at the rocks, and a silvery pompano can perhaps be seen gliding nearby. Groups of squid are not unusual in our waters and, with a bit of patience, an occasional octopus might be seen. Probably the most delightful aspect of strolling along the beaches and shoreline is that everything is perfectly safe; dangerous species such as sharks traditionally prowl the ocean beyond the protective reefs.

The vast majority of Bermuda's public beaches sprawl picturesquely along the **South Shore**, the majority in the parishes of **Paget, Warwick** and **Southampton**. It is in this area that the island's celebrated **pink sands** can be seen at their finest, as long beaches and smaller coves alternate with one another for mile after mile. Among the more famous beaches are **Horseshoe Bay, Warwick Long Bay, Chaplin Bay** and **Jobson Cove**. They are all readily accessible from the main South Road and can be clearly seen from viewing bays along the roadside. Parking spaces are available for bikes and cars at each of the main beach areas. **Horseshoe Bay** is something of a focal point for several adjacent smaller beaches; here there is the **Beach House** which offers shower facilities and a delightful dining area serving snacks, drinks and various sundries.

Devil's Hole. (DAVID F. RAINE)

Whereas this is the longest stretch of coastline with beaches, all of Bermuda's beaches offer their own sense of beauty and charm. Towards the eastern end **John Smith's Bay** is just round the corner from the **Devil's Hole**, and offers rocks to explore, two sandy beaches to lie on and the splendid vista of waves breaking over the offshore reefs. A lunch wagon in the nearby parking lot offers excellent snacks. In Sandys Parish, **Mangrove Bay** is surely among the most picturesque beaches in Bermuda, with its crescented shape rimmed by slender, swaying palms; fishing boats and smaller punts lie peacefully at anchor in the shallow waters and contribute to the tranquillity of the scene. Located off the main road in **Somerset Village**, its close proximity to the shops makes it additionally convenient for food, film and sundry other beach needs.

At the other end of Bermuda, the most famous public beach is undoubtedly at **Tobacco Bay**, on the northern side of St George's island. The waters are shallow and ideal for families, whilst there are also some fascinating rock formations and natural pools to keep adults busy for hours. A privately-operated beach house, very personally run by the ever popular Kenny Bacombe, provides everything from drinks to snorkelling equipment. Small boats may be rented — and he'll even lend you a book to read! Incidentally, this area is perhaps one of the best spots in Bermuda for amateur or avid snorkellers: dive in at the mouth of adjacent **Coot Pond** and all manner of harmless water creatures and fishes will soon be seen.

For those seeking to get closer to Bermuda's deeper waters, several companies operate regular glass-bottom boat trips out to various sections of the reef. Under the direction of an experienced captain and guide, those totally unfamiliar with what lies below the waves will get a really worthwhile exposure to the beauty of Bermuda's underwater world. Here purple and green corals and bright orange sponges become the natural setting for many varieties of our native tropical fish. Large snappers, bream and grunts are very common, but the more fortunate may even catch a glimpse of hinds, coney, mackerel, ocean robins and possibly a stray shark or barracuda.

Diving amongst Bermuda's coral. (BERMUDA TOURISM)

Depending on the route taken by each boat, those venturing further out may even see flying fish. The glass-bottom boat which operates out of St George's also tries to include a pause over the 1609 wreck of the *Sea Venture*; however, as with all such trips, much depends upon the continuously changing conditions of the sea and ocean floor on any given day.

There are also two somewhat unusual experiences awaiting those who may be slightly more adventurous or curious about Bermuda's underwater sights: a submarine dive off the **West End**, or helmet-diving out of **Flatts Inlet**. Bermuda's submarine is one of only two such vessels operating in this part of the world and several dives are made daily throughout most of the year. Passengers are taken from the quayside in the Dockyard aboard a luxury tender and are then transferred on to the submarine at a location just off **Ireland Island**. Dives last for roughly half an hour and cost approximately $50 per person. Equally unusual is helmet-diving, which involves being taken beneath the waters somewhere off **Shelley Bay** for a most stimulating stroll along the ocean floor. Each small group is personally escorted by famous diver Bronson Hartley, who most informatively points out various fish and corals, whilst also providing a demonstration to show how sponges breathe. His half-day excursions cost about $30 and include underwater video shows on board to entertain those waiting to don helmets and descend.

Anyone with a penchant for deep-sea fishing can easily do it from docks all around the shore. The Bermuda Government is very careful to grant permits only to those charter captains who have met very stringent requirements. Not only is each boat checked annually for seaworthiness and safety, but the captains themselves must also be holders of an authorised pilot's certificate awarded by the Department of Marine and Port Services. Charges are made by the half-day or full-day and are usually quoted at a capacity rate for six persons. The **Bermuda Charter Fishermen's Association** can furnish details on boat availability, costs and the type of fish most likely to be caught at specific offshore sites. Captains are very accommodating and will troll for marlin, wahoo, tuna, bonefish and bonito just as willingly as they will drop anchor off the outer reefs and let fishermen try their luck for shark, porgy, moray eels, hind, barracuda and amberjacks.

The **Government Aquarium**, in Flatts, provides the ideal venue to gaze at Bermuda's underwater wildlife from the stability of terra firma! Open just about every day of the year except for Christmas Day, the aquarium offers a very full display of almost everything which can be found in local waters. All fish species on exhibition have been caught by local fishermen, or by the facility's own boating staff; the living corals, anemones, lobsters, eels and octopi have likewise been brought up from our own waters. Each tank is clearly labelled and 'tour wands' are available without charge for those wishing to learn just a little more about the exhibits. To the rear of the main house there is a small museum with displays relating to Bermuda's volcanic origins, the whaling industry, corals, fossils and a glimpse of the work done on Bermuda by William Beebe, the true pioneer of underwater research. In the gardens out at the back is a small zoo containing Galapagos tortoises and flamingoes bred in Bermuda, as well as a miscellany of exotic birds, lemurs, alligators, turtles and lizards.

Just a few minutes from Flatts, along the **Harrington Sound Road**, is the celebrated **Devil's Hole**, a small natural grotto in which a splendid array of groupers, angelfish, snappers and hind swim freely within a collapsed cave, among sharks, eels and turtles. An oft-quoted story has it that the legendary swimming star Esther Williams once dropped her purse overboard while on a visit here. With brazen spirit, and apparently not much sense, she reputedly dived in to retrieve it — a plunge which took her simultaneously into the sharks and also into local folklore.

Opposite the airport, at Ferry Reach, is the **Bermuda Biological Station for Research**, a scientific institute founded in 1903. Bermuda's unusual position, firmly perched atop a volcano which erupted on the deepest floor of the Atlantic Ocean, has made it a favourite site from which scientists may conduct research into all manner of oceanographic topics. Using the stations's own ocean-going vessels, researchers can find themselves probing the ocean's greatest depths far quicker and with greater confidence than if they had to spend time crossing the broad continental shelves first, as happens elsewhere.

Bermuda was the place that Dr William Beebe chose sixty years ago as the site for his historic bathysphere dives into the unexplored darkness of the Atlantic — a full twenty years, incidentally, before Jacques Cousteau began working with aqua-lung devices for far shallower dives. In his wake, quite literally, has come a flood of scientists seeking to understand more about the unsolved mysteries of the ocean. Their work has contributed to world knowledge in such diversified areas as coral bleaching, nutrient limitations and sponge development; from the reproductive behaviour of microscopic organisms and flatworm studies, to wider issues such as monitoring air and water pollution. It was from here that a team of underwater explorers recently discovered and photographed the hitherto unknown six-gilled shark; how many other fresh discoveries have been made from here is probably incalculable.

The Biological Station provides research and accommodation facilities for groups of scientific investigators from all over the world. Any serious researchers are welcome to apply for permission to use the centre's private library; tours are arranged for members of the general public on a regular basis. Any questions relating to this fascinating facility can be answered by its always helpful staff, over the telephone or by mail.

If watery topics are of no interest, then those preferring to stay more firmly on dry land will be satisfied in countless other ways. Travelling around Bermuda is very simple, even though non-residents are not permitted to rent private cars. For upwards of about $20 per day, depending on the length of time required, visitors may rent an auxiliary bicycle and travel the country's highways and byeways with total freedom. Bermuda is only twenty-one square miles in total area, so it is virtually impossible to get lost. Once mobile, there is much to discover with the help of a basic fold-up map given away by the Tourism Department. There are reliable buses and ferries too, with regularly scheduled services to all parts of the country. They are not only a comfortable means of transport, but are also relatively inexpensive to use. Brochures detailing times and frequencies on each system can be acquired from the Hamilton bus terminal on Church Street, or from the main ferry terminal on Front Street.

Bermudians use the ferries for their daily commuting to and from work. The system operates solely within the limits of Hamilton Harbour, but because of the configuration of the coastline this automatically means connections all the way along the opposite shores of Paget and Warwick, and right on up into the Dockyard. Visitors staying

Visitors can take a ride in a horse-driven buggy if cycling doesn't appeal.
(BERMUDA TOURISM)

Cyclists stop for a rest under a moongate. (BERMUDA TOURISM)

at hotels and guest houses in any of these parishes would do well to enquire about the nearest ferry stop, as a pleasant way of travelling around the country. The service is inexpensive and offers an ideal way to pass among the islands and bays of the Great Sound. There is also a provision for passengers to take bikes on board, thus giving the traveller the option of returning either by land or water.

Points of historical interest are scattered from one end of Bermuda to the other. The Dockyard area, mentioned elsewhere in greater detail, is always worth a visit and, depending upon when and where the day begins other historic sites can be visited on the way. Many of the island's fortifications date back into the seventeenth century and most are quite accessible. **Fort Scaur** and **Fort Hamilton**, in particular, afford outstanding panoramic views over Hamilton Harbour in addition to providing the opportunity to explore two of the most picturesque settings in which any military forts have been built. The same might also be said for **Fort St Catherine**, which was built

Verdmont interior. (BERMUDA TOURISM)

on a promontory behind St George. Constructed mainly in the nineteenth century, when the British Empire was reaching a peak of expansive confidence, this is one of the largest fortifications in Bermuda, offering today's visitor a seemingly endless network of underground rooms and walkways in which are exhibited uniforms, rifles and other forms of weaponry from another era. There is also a chamber which displays replicas of the British Crown Jewels. Unless you have your own transport, the easiest way to get to Fort St Catherine is by the town's mini-bus service, which can be picked-up in King's Square; it is within walking distance, but can be dehydrating on a summer's day!

The Bermuda National Trust maintains several fine old Bermudian homes which the general public is encouraged to visit. Probably the most impressive of these is **Verdmont**, just off Middle Road, in Smith's Parish. This splendid structure is one of the best preserved domestic homes from the seventeenth century; each of the rooms is carefully furnished and decorated down to the finest details of curtains, quilts, knives and forks, cooking ware and original portraits. For a nominal fee, regular and personal guided tours are available without prior reservation. The house is elegantly set in its own manicured grounds and much of the plant life is that which would have been growing on the original estate.

Other National Trust properties which warrant a visit are the **Confederate Museum**, **Tucker House** and **Bridge House**, all in St George. The former was once the home of a Major Walker, who was actually the official confederate agent permanently stationed in Bermuda during the American Civil War. It would seem that the island's entrepreneurs fared quite well during that troubled period on the mainland, as they conveniently and delicately acted as intermediaries between trading partners for both sides, as well as indirectly between the warring North and South themselves! Tucker House and Bridge House were both private houses. The former has become a delightful museum whilst the latter is probably Bermuda's oldest surviving private residence, in that it continues to be used as such. Today it is internally divided into three units, two of which are private apartments. The third area is used for the **Bridge House Art Gallery** — Bermuda's leading centre for locally-made arts and crafts. Just round the corner is the St George's **Historical Society Museum**, laid-out with original furnishings from several hundred years ago.

The Bermuda National Trust maintains close links with similar bodies throughout the world and it is worthwhile knowing that membership in one National Trust customarily grants entrance concessions among the others. The headquarters in Bermuda are located in the elegant house named **Waterville**, which is along the Harbour Road in Paget, a short walk from the roundabout at the Foot-of-the-Lane, in Hamilton.

In St George, it is worthwhile stopping to look through **St Peter's Church**. Situated near the site of the first church built on these islands in 1610, it enjoys the reputation of being the oldest continuously used Anglican church in the western hemisphere. In addition to the fine cedar woodwork and beams, it is worth taking time to admire

Overleaf: *Crystal Cave.* (BERMUDA TOURISM)

the small but fine collection of silver in the ante-room. Many international figures have paused to worship here, including Queen Elizabeth and most members of her family, Presidents Eisenhower, Kennedy and Nixon and many other world personalities. In the adjacent cemetery can be found the graves of several prominent Bermudian, British and North American personages who have died on these shores. Included among these is Sir Richard Sharples who has the dubious place in local history of being the first and only Governor ever to have been assassinated in Bermuda. The **Rectory** of St Peter's is just out of the back gates. Presently administered by the Bermuda National Trust, the Rectory is leased as a private home but is open to the public on specific days each week.

Another island spot worth a visit is the **Perfume Factory**, at Bailey's Bay, where perfumes are made from locally-grown flowers. Also in Bailey's Bay there are two caves open to the public — **Crystal Cave** and **Leamington Cave**. Both are along the Harrington Sound Road and offer guided tours on a daily basis.

For those inclined towards the outdoors, the Government maintains parks throughout the length and breadth of Bermuda. Most of these have clearly marked trails or paths to enable visitors to walk into the more interesting areas of what we like to describe as 'unspoilt' land. Additionally, the Bermuda National Trust and the Audubon Society are responsible for various Nature Reserves located in each Parish, protected parcels of land which not only assure the retention of the natural vegetation, but which also attract hundreds of migrant birds each year.

Bermudians, it is often said, enjoy life because they have managed to create a fine balance between work and play. They have also succeeded in keeping hold of what they have, retaining a legacy on land and sea which will continue to interest others for many generations to come.

| 15 |
Enjoying a night out...

It is difficult to imagine a more idyllic setting for a pleasant night of relaxation and entertainment than one which begins with the yellows and pinks of a Bermuda sunset and then warmly continues beneath clear, starry skies; a gentle breeze wafting from the ocean. Bermuda really does offer such a setting throughout much of the year.

Of course, on such nights many people prefer to pass the time quietly listening to the sounds of rolling waves, or going for a leisurely stroll, with tiny tree frogs furnishing a background of natural music. There are others, however, who may also wish to join the throngs of Bermudians who enjoy what is somewhat loosely described as 'a night out': a good meal, served in gracious surroundings, followed by some sort of live entertainment.

On these islands, there is never any shortage of places to go for a truly memorable supper. Bermuda is well-known for having more than its fair share of world-renowned restaurants and dining-rooms, spanning the international cuisine of every continent sufficiently to satisfy even the most fastidious of palates. Many of the major hotel dining-rooms are open to members of the public, although prior reservations are invariably required.

The **Princess Hotels** in both Hamilton and Southampton have always attracted gourmets and, like the **Elbow Beach Hotel**, they employ chefs who have won culinary awards both here and overseas. Marriott's **Castle Harbour** has, in particular, an outstanding Japanese restaurant called **The Mikado**, in which all food is prepared

Princess Hotel, Hamilton. (BERMUDA TOURISM)

The Plantation. (DAVID F. RAINE)

at the table by experts whose skills go far beyond mere preparation and cooking to include a fascinating juggling display with their kitchen utensils. **The Norwood Room**, in the **Bermuda Government's Hotel Training College** at Stonington Beach, in Paget, is also very popular among visitors and residents alike. Here, under the watchful eye of their tutors, students prepare and serve meals of unquestionably high standard, and the cheque at the end is pleasantly reasonable.

Those seeking a truly luxurious dining experience should consider a visit to **Fourways**, in Paget, **Tom Moore's Tavern** or **The Plantation** nearby; the latter two are both in Smith's Parish. Each of these offers excellent food and enjoys the unique setting of an old Bermuda home — the Tavern, in fact, was formerly a private home named 'Walsingham', frequented by the Irish poet Tom Moore during a six-month sojourn here in 1804. In Sandys Parish, **Loyalty Inn** provides a more general and less expensive menu, but the restaurant is also in a fascinating old home; it is particularly popular for fish and steak meals. In the Towne of St George, along Water Street, outstanding à la carte evening meals are impeccably served amidst elegant surroundings at **The Carriage House**; this was once an eighteenth century waterfront warehouse, but it has long since been refurbished to accommodate a friendly and spacious restaurant. **The Pub on the Square**, also in the Olde Towne, is somewhat less formal but offers a general menu and a pleasing view of the harbour for those who can manage to reserve a table on the verandah.

Within the City of Hamilton, there is a variety of restaurants adequate enough to satisfy all tastes and pockets. For those looking for a relaxing lunch or supper, complete with full table service, there are several excellent places to choose from. On Front Street, **The Harbourfront** affords generous views over Hamilton Harbour and a fine menu. Close by, **Loquats** and **The Conchshell** also enjoy considerable popularity among locals and visitors alike for the high quality of food and service. On Reid Street, in the old Armoury Building, there is **The Red Carpet** which, although somewhat small, offers an impressive variety of foods and an equally impressive wine list. One block up, on Church Street, **Romanoff** has secured a loyal clientele as much for its distinctly courteous European service as for its *haute cuisine*. For those with a penchant for Italian dishes, **La Trattoria**, in Washington Lane, presents a very broad selection of dishes, especially in salads and pastas. Just outside Hamilton, in the heart of the Botanical Gardens, the aptly named **Tavern on the Green** enjoys a truly unique setting to compliment its broad and distinguished menu. Up at the Dockyard **The Blue Oyster** offers a relaxed atmosphere and a cuisine which inclines towards the French.

For entertainment after a meal, the main hotels are an obvious place to start exploring. Most feature some form of live entertainment and local newspapers are the best source for identifying specific acts which might be featured on any given night of the week. Featured performers are both local and foreign.

Those wanting to enjoy a bit of local jazz might do as well to try to find out where Shine Hayward or Ghandi Burgess are playing; these two jazz performers are recognised as the real giants among local musicians and attract the cream of Bermudian talent into various supporting musical ensembles. Calypso lovers should seek out Hubert Smith or the legendary Talbot Brothers, each of whom has been composing music and recording albums for several decades. Hubert Smith was the composer of the song 'Bermuda is another world', a number which has become an anthem-like standard for all local calypsonians. The Talbot Brothers offer a slightly more traditional style of calypso, with all rhythms set to the beat of their legendary tea-chest bass. Among the tunes most frequently requested, they perform a particularly moving rendition of the classic 'Ebb Tide' which is always well worth waiting for.

The Strollers are another Bermudian act which should not be missed. They perform in a variety of different locations and offer an exciting and energetic type of entertainment incorporating a musical repertoire which flows easily from ballads, to calypso and on into more contemporary and upbeat rhythms. They have frequently gone on promotional tours with the Department of Tourism and this, combined with their popularity during the annual College Weeks has brought them a considerable international following. Solo performers, duos and groups can be found in the vast majority of the smaller restaurants and pubs, so that most tastes are catered for whether they are for the soothing sounds of a solitary piano, calypso, the folksy tunes of a guitar, or the somewhat more raucous beats of a hearty 'sing-along'.

On Front Street, in Hamilton, younger couples will find continuous dancing and entertainment in the famous **Disco Forty**, complete with flashing strobe lighting and music video screens. In previous decades the club had a reputation as the place where celebrities such as Dionne Warwick and Tom Jones would take to the stage. However, that supper-club image has long since changed and the nightclub has now become one of the premier venues for the best in pop, rock and reggae. On Middle Road in Warwick, the slightly smaller club named **Flavours** provides a most worthy alternative for the same type of clientele, with continuous music and dancing offered in a discotheque atmosphere. **The Spinning Wheel**, on Court Street in Hamilton, will amply satisfy those with a yearning to dance or listen to reggae, soul and pop music. Live acts alternate with the sounds provided by a resident deejay.

Anyone looking for the more traditional form of musical entravaganza featuring a

The Strollers. (DEPARTMENT OF TOURISM, BERMUDA)

chorus line, dazzling costumes and plenty of bright lights, should head for the **Southampton Princess Hotel** which has gradually become the established home of a spectacular revue by 'The Follies'. This show features an almost continuous parade of Bermudian and visiting dancers, singers and entertainers, and is quite unlike anything offered anywhere else on these islands. Of the so-called 'native' shows, the best is probably the one staged nightly at the **Clayhouse Inn**, about ten minutes' ride from Hamilton, along the North Shore in Devonshire. Here, lovers of the steel band can sit and listen to the rhythms of some of Bermuda's finest players, when 'The Coca Cola Steel Band'. performs a variety of music ranging from calypso, to pop and on into Handel's 'Hallelujah Chorus'. Incidentally, the latter is especially delightful if listened to from the rear patio, with the sounds gently drifting off the adjacent waterfront and out to sea. Calypso singers, congo drummers and limbo dancers are also invariably included in each of the nightly shows.

During the months of January and February, visitors should be aware that Bermuda stages its own Festival. This is a time when international artists from all realms of the performing arts are invited to appear. It is an occasion for plays, ballet, modern dance, opera, classical guitar, string and jazz quartets and madrigal singers to participate in a very high level of entertainment. Details of what might be expected during any forthcoming season can be obtained by contacting the offices of The Bermuda Festival, in the Chamber of Commerce Building, on Front Street in Hamilton.

Finally, Bermuda offers three cinemas, each showing regularly advertised programmes of the most up-to-date movies. The newest of these is the **Neptune Cinema**, located up in the Dockyard, in Somerset. The **Little Theatre** and the **Liberty Theatre** are in Hamilton.

Irrespective of individual tastes in dining and entertainment, Bermuda has a wealth of talent and a host of facilities to satisfy anyone's desire to have a full and enjoyable 'night out' — especially on those warm evenings when the breeze is gently wafting across the water and the waves are breaking on a secluded beach . . .

| 16 |
Protecting this natural beauty

Alongside the friendliness of her people, one of Bermuda's greatest assets is her natural beauty. It abounds everywhere. You can see it among the scattered islands of the Great Sound; it sparkles in the crystal waters of Horseshoe Bay; it lies in the quietness of a secluded beach, the sight of the sun rising through a moongate and the memory of sunset at Flatts.

In an age when the rest of the world is bemoaning the widescale loss of natural vegetation and the unending mutilation of the planet's landscape, it should be encouraging to realise that Bermuda has been protecting its environment for nearly four hundred years. Indeed, early Bermudian legislators enacted such a thoughtfully interwoven network of laws that they were surely among the true pioneers of environmental protection.

Nature, of course, has automatically imposed her own series of natural laws upon these islands. By virtue of their isolation and being a very small area of fragmented land, configured in such a way as to deny inhabitants any 'interior' whatsoever, Bermudians have historically been compelled to live in harmony with each other, and their natural environment. Indeed, these natural laws fell irreversibly into place even whilst the original settlers were still unpacking their cabin trunks. It was inevitable, for example, that islands devoid of any significant amount of freshwater should immediately seek to protect themselves against the careless or deliberate pollution of existing sources. Equally apparent was the absence of a hinterland with limitless forests; therefore timber, too, would need to be conserved. Similarly, the wilful destruction of birds' eggs and other food supplies was clearly a life-threatening act of sabotage against which everyone needed to be defended.

When the first Assembly of local representatives was officially convened in 1620, these natural laws were promptly passed into formal legislation. Over the years they have been regularly augmented by others and now constitute not only the laws of this land, but represent an historic landmark in the annals of environmental protection.

From the outset, Bermudians blended their experiences with an inherent sensitivity, to produce sweeping pieces of legislation which collectively strove to conserve all of these islands' natural resources. For example, as the direct result of the famine of 1614, they were abruptly alerted to the potential dangers of the unregulated slaughtering of wildlife. Very quickly, therefore, various fish, most birds and all turtles, became protected under law. Younger turtles were particularly safeguarded when it became an offence to kill any turtles 'within five leagues of the coast' if their shells

Overleaf: *Castle Island — an illustration of Bermuda's spectacular natural beauty.*
(BERMUDA TOURISM)

were less than eighteen inches in diameter. To this day, it remains illegal deliberately to kill any turtles within Bermudian territorial waters.

Fish have always been singled out for protection. The very first two Governors issued what they not so subtly described as 'forceful instructions' relating to the use of bait-nets and the avoidance of undue wastage from catches. These were followed by a strictly-enforced fishing code which perceptively acknowledged the significance of smaller bait-fish in the overall feeding chain of the larger species. One law passed in 1627, for example, unequivocally prohibited the catching of either fry or pilchard for the purpose of making oil for lamps and other non-essentials. Records from another early seventeenth-century debate refer to the fact that overkilling small fish would inevitably result in 'chasing away other greate fish from the shoars'; 'breame and the suchlike' were consequently brought under the protection of the law. Incidentally, infringements of these measures were not taken lightly and involved confiscation of nets, plus the imposing of tobacco fines — a commodity which was virtually Bermuda's main currency at that time!

In keeping with the early protective spirit toward sea-life, fishing remains the subject of endless rules and regulations. There are areas off the shore which have been determined to be the natural breeding grounds of the speckled hind, and in these marked zones fishing is completely prohibited. All commercial and charter fishermen must be licensed and they are obliged to record their catches on a daily log-sheet. This is then submitted to the Government department which monitors fish stocks. It is illegal for anyone else to sell fish. Persons wishing to use fish-pots cannot do so unless they have a permit; even then, the number is stipulated, as are clear specifications as to size and the construction materials which may be used for each pot. Foreign vessels fishing commercially in these waters must secure an authorisation from the Bermuda Government.

Birds were also severely over-hunted by the first settlers and natural supplies of petrels, cahows and herons became so obviously depleted that laws were soon passed to protect them and their eggs. In 1622, severe restrictions were imposed on the killing of any birds during their annual breeding periods and measures quickly followed seeking to impose limits on how many each hunter could claim. Similar measures were taken to discourage the killing of any birds on the outer islands — thereby creating the forerunners of our present wildlife sanctuaries and nature reserves. Other islands were decreed to be 'Commonland' — a legal expression used in England to designate property to be owned by the public in perpetuity. Thus began a tradition which has produced many public parks throughout Bermuda today. These areas are destined to be forever protected from the ravages of bull-dozers and housing developments.

Perhaps time did eventually prove that these efforts were inadequate to prevent the near-extinction of the cahow, but that bird still continues to be protected under Bermuda law and a small colony is now gradually being re-established — the only place, we might note, in the entire world where this species has survived. In fact, contemporary legislation prohibits the use of all firearms in Bermuda and there continues to be a complete abhorrence for the killing of any birds. This was especially manifested just a few years ago when the Government Conservation Officer received permission to shoot a solitary snowy owl which had been inadvertently blown here from the Arctic during a storm and which had been spotted killing some treasured cahow chicks. The uproar created by the eventual death of this one bird lasted for several weeks. There is always an instinctive twinge of sadness at the sight of a dead longtail in the road, or a cormorant damaged by high wires. In Bermuda, birds were meant to live in harmony with man.

Although they have long since been wiped out, even the abundant wild hog was embraced by protective laws as far back as 1623. Thereafter, it became incumbent on any hunter to prove that he genuinely intended to utilise the animal to the fullest, before he was permitted to kill it. Some segments of the community regarded this as being entirely nonsensical because roaming hogs were recognised island-wide as nuisances which damaged crops and freshly-planted saplings. However, the law also recognised that those self-same swine were also an important natural food source, and deserved protection from wanton, unbridled killing. Those who ignored the laws were not only fined, but the carcass of the unfortunate beast was confiscated by the neighbourhood constable and freely distributed to the needy. Alas! today, hogs survive only on the obverse side of the one cent coin, but no one can say that we didn't try to protect them!

The preservation of natural vegetation has always been a major concern in Bermuda and the rapid destruction of the cedar and palmetto forests was a target for immediate concern among the early settlers. Trees, for sure, had to be felled for such purposes as home and boat-building, but even these legitimate demands had soon drastically thinned St George's Island of its natural vegetation. A relatively prompt solution was forthcoming, and in 1620 legislation was passed requiring that new seedlings be planted each time a mature tree was felled. This policy was reinforced by the Timber Preservation Act of 1627 and seems to have been remarkably farsighted particularly when compared to the denuded state of Europe during that same era. Clearly Bermuda was ahead of its time in implementing a programme of re-afforestation! Somewhat characteristically, it seems, the environmentally-conscious settlers took an extra step and passed a further law obliging turkey owners to corral 'them and other fowl'; evidently their high-powered beaks and claws were proving to be a severe threat to younger plants and crops. (As an overt inducement to honour the law, a sub-clause was inserted, allowing that all roaming 'fowle' be confiscated by their finders and 'taken away to the pot'.)

The exportation of cabin trunks and furniture made from local cedar was prohibited during the embryonic stages of Bermuda's legal history, recognising that any manufacturing industry based upon the islands' limited natural resources was destined to precipitate long-term harm to the environment. Tragically, by a sad stroke of irony, the cedar trees were finally felled not by man but by an insect blight in the 1940s and their numbers will not recover from this drastic decimation for several generations. Nevertheless, it continues to be a serious offence to cut down cedar trees that don't belong to you and those that have a preservation order on them.

A similarly outraged attitude once prevailed towards tampering with tobacco plants. Stealing, uprooting and causing damage to these and other crops was regarded as

The Headquarters of the Bermuda National Trust. (MICHAEL BOURNE)

a serious crime against the cultivated landscape. The law also forbade the taking of short-cuts across private property, because it was felt that these unnecessary man-made paths became offensive scars on the natural environment. A contemporary parallel persists today, with controls which are strictly applied to horse and motor-cross trails.

Each one of these, sometimes obscure, passages of legislation was an integral part of a remarkable and comprehensive package of laws which, by 1630, had gone a long way towards laying permanent and protective foundations beneath the entire natural environment of Bermuda. Furthermore, those early efforts were directly responsible for fostering a tradition of true concern which has been transmitted through generations of Bermudians, right up to the present time. Today they continue to be instinctively protective towards all facets of the natural beauty of their surroundings.

At the present time there is a moratorium on the harvesting of conch, calico clams and several other species of shellfish, to be held in place until such times as depleted stocks are naturally re-established. The hunting of turtles is banned unconditionally, and many decades have already slipped by since any Bermudian whalers launched their longboats and chased that mighty mammal. The former whaling house on Smith's Island has long since been converted into a family residence and the descendants of old-time whalers now watch instead from dry land, fascinated as pods of humpbacks blow and frolic off the South Shore during their yearly April-May migration. The oil cauldrons and rusty harpoons are on display in museums.

The land of these islands is today guarded with both caution and jealousy. Quarrying limestone to make building-blocks for homes and walls requires a licence, and a declaration that consequent excavations will not destroy the natural skyline. Policy also demands that buildings should not infringe upon those same land horizons either. Pollution of both sea and atmosphere are also encompassed by Bermuda's Law Books — and even some of the world's finest cruise ships, a lifeline in the vital tourist industry, have been brought before the local courts for releasing oil slicks or causing unsightly and odorous smoke emissions.

Laws have also been enacted to stop preventable damage to the natural shoreline: neither walls nor docks can be built until a Government committee has approved construction techniques and the final appearance of what will be produced. Indeed there was considerable reaction from Bermudians in 1986 when one major hotel sought to erect a simple wooden duckboard between its beach and docking facilities; it was an instinctive response, based upon concern over the potential disruption to the ecology of that short section of coast. The plan was modified and the walkway was duly elevated out of harm's way.

There are many public watch-dog committees, most operating through the broadening scope of the increasingly vocal Bermuda National Trust, which reports on everything from potential damage caused by Government road-widening projects, through to noise pollution, building extensions, changes in land-use and littering. It was indeed a significant reflection of these concerns that Stuart Hayward was elected as an Independent Member of Parliament in 1989, after standing for office on a platform which was perceived to be based substantially upon environmental issues.

Bermuda is unique, and it is indeed a grouping of some of the most beautiful islands in the world. Hopefully, future generations will guard them with the same zealousness as have their predecessors.

| 17 |
Bermuda and the sporting life

Bermudians are great lovers of the outdoors and engage in a whole range of sporting activities throughout the year. As is generally the case in other parts of the world, most sports are seasonal. The following is a list of the most common sporting and allied activities complete with addresses and telephone numbers where representatives may be contacted.

The Bermuda Amateur Swimming Association
c/o The Saltus Swimming Pool,
Saltus Grammar School,
St John's Road, Pembroke
Tel: 292 – 1713

The majority of Bermudians are as at home in the water as they are on the land. They have been participating in local and overseas meets for decades and have sent representatives to participate in regional competitions, as well as the Olympic and Commonwealth Games. There are several clubs and they arrange competitions for their own members, as well as competing against one another and visiting teams from abroad.

Bermuda Bicycle Association
Court Street,
Hamilton
Tel: 295 – 9972

This sport continues to attract an ever-growing following, with the result that many closed-circuit and road-races are now featured on the Association's calendar during the course of each year. Members have competed overseas, both in North America and in Europe, and national teams have participated in the Olympic Games.

Bermuda Boat and Canoe Club
Pembroke
Tel: 295 – 6904

This is essentially a small group of enthusiasts who organise outings for their members during the summer months and on weekends. Activities centre primarily on in-shore canoe excursions. Since some members have made their own canoes they have often given construction advice and technique demonstrations to youngsters at the Government-sponsored summer camps.

Bermuda Bridge Club
Pomander Road,
Paget
Tel: 236 – 0551

Bermuda has a very active association with various Bridge clubs throughout the world and frequently hosts tournaments locally, as well as sending players to compete overseas. Members hold regular intra-club sessions and top players take part in all levels of international events.

Bermuda Cricket Board of Control
Park House,
Hamilton
Tel: 295 – 1826

Cricket is the main sport during the summer months. There is a variety of leagues and divisions for teams competing at all levels and all local schools have at least one competitive cricket team. Overseas tours are often arranged for the national team, as well as club and school teams. Bermuda frequently plays host to visiting cricketers from other parts of the world and at least two prominent players have gone on to play cricket professionally in Britain: Alma 'Champ' Hunt and perhaps our greatest all-rounder, Clarence Parfitt.

Bermuda Darts Association
Smith's Parish
Tel: 293 – 1446

Darts is a very popular game. Most of the Working Men's clubs have teams which compete in the main league. Several pubs and various other sporting clubs also organise competitions for their clientele and general membership, and many take part in island-wide competitions. Exhibition matches are arranged with visiting players of international repute and local players have participated in regional events.

Bermuda Football Association
Par-la-Ville Road,
Hamilton
Tel: 295 – 2199

Football, known elsewhere as soccer, is Bermuda's national winter pastime. There are many teams incorporated into a network of various leagues and divisions which span from junior school level right on up to the national squad. Whilst all locals are part-time players, they often compete in friendly matches against visiting professional teams from Europe. Bermuda regularly participates in international competitions, including regional and Olympic qualifying events, and is a former Commonwealth Games silver medallist. Since the 1960s several players have turned professional by joining teams in England and North America. The most illustrious of these was Clyde Best, whose professional career spanned the 1970s and saw him become a leading goalscorer in the English First Division, whilst with West Ham. He subsequently played in Dutch, American and Canadian teams before retiring.

Bermuda Golf Association
Warwick
Tel: 293 – 1446

Proudly claiming to have some of the most picturesque golf courses in the world, Bermuda also possesses some of the most challenging ones — in both the public and private sectors. A variety of pro-am tournaments are arranged throughout the year by individual clubs and also by privately-sponsored organisations. There is a regular exchange of teams and players on an international level, with Bermudians of all ages and abilities taking part.

The islands' golf clubs are:

Belmont Hotel and Golf Club, Warwick	Tel: 236 – 2095
Marriott's Castle Harbour Golf Club, Tucker's Town	Tel: 293 – 0795
Mid Ocean Club, Tucker's Town	Tel: 293 – 0330
Port Royal Golf Course, Southampton	Tel: 234 – 0974
Queen's Park Golf Club, Devonshire	Tel: 236 – 6758
Riddell's Bay Golf and Country Club, Warwick	Tel: 238 – 1060
Southampton Princess Golf Club, Southampton	Tel: 238 – 0446
St George's Golf Club, St George	Tel: 297 – 8067

Bermuda Horse and Pony Association
Smith's Parish
Tel: 292 – 5222

There are several privately-run stables in Bermuda which arrange regular training classes for members, in addition to renting horses and equipment to visitors. Competitions are held at various times throughout the year which, whilst primarily for local participants, also attract foreign entrants. Bermudians have entered events overseas and have also participated in the Olympic Games.

Bermuda Kennel Club Inc.

P.O. Box HM 1455,
Hamilton
Tel: 238 – 0772

This has a very active membership which, after many years of hard work, now arranges training sessions and several shows each year. The club also regularly hosts one of the region's major international dog shows, attracting judges and breeders from throughout North America.

Bermuda Lawn Tennis Association

c/o The National Tennis Stadium,
2 Marsh Folly Road,
Pembroke HM 13
Tel: 292 – 0105

Tennis is very popular in Bermuda both as a spectator and participant sport. It is played throughout the year. Although most hotels have their own private courts, anyone is welcome to book games through the Tennis Stadium. All are floodlit for night play. Several local clubs organise their own competitions and many attract overseas players. Ranked Bermudian players have also entered various international professional and amateur tournaments, including those at regional and Olympic levels.

The Martial Arts

There are three main schools in Bermuda which teach the martial arts. Each is directed by an internationally-recognised master. Students participate in tournaments both at home and overseas and competitions are arranged at both amateur and professional levels. Annual Invitational Championships are arranged for locals and invited participants from abroad. The schools are:

The Bermuda Karate Institute, 54 Court Street, Hamilton
Tel: 292 – 2157

The Bermuda Shotokan Karate, St John's Road, Pembroke
Tel: 295 – 0282

The Bermuda Tae Kwon Do Association, Deep Bay, Pembroke.
Tel: 292 – 8170

Overleaf: *Mid Ocean Golf Club.* (BERMUDA TOURISM)

Bermuda Rugby Federation
c/o National Sports Club,
Middle Road,
Devonshire
Tel: 236 – 6994

Rugby has been a major winter sport in Bermuda for decades, and it enjoys popularity not only at club level but also within many schools. Competitions are held on a league basis, but various knock-out events are also staged. In recent years Bermuda has become the regular host for visiting foreign teams and groups from Bermuda travel overseas. Since November 1988, a major international tournament has been attracting star players from all over the world who compete in national teams for a final championship trophy. This extravaganza was primarily the brain-child of Fraser Butterworth and John Kane, two players with a team appropriately named 'Old Bermuda', who successfully sought to enhance the enjoyment of local rugby for spectators and players alike.

Bermuda Softball Association
c/o The Softball Stadium,
Barnard Park,
2 Marsh Folly Road,
Pembroke
Tel: 292 – 3749

There are many teams playing this sport in Bermuda and considerable success has been won by those representing the country in international competitions. For most of the 1970s regional international meets were totally dominated by Bermuda's legendary 'Big Blue Machine', a group of female players who filled their cabinets with almost every available trophy. In addition to regular league fixtures, the Association also arranges training sessions for players and organises courses for referees.

Bermuda Special Olympics
Court Street,
Hamilton
Tel: 292 – 7481

This is a group consisting mainly of volunteers dedicated to encouraging Bermudians with various physical and mental handicaps to compete against themselves and each other in a wide range of athletic activities. Teams have regularly been sent overseas to participate in the world-wide Special Olympics programme and, over the years, local athletes have returned from these international events with many medals and awards.

The National Tennis Stadium. (BERMUDA TOURISM)

Bermuda Squash Racquets Association
Middle Road,
Devonshire
Tel: 292 – 6881

Most of the activities centre upon the main courts built by the Association adjacent to National Sports Club facilities, in Devonshire. Members can book games any day of the week for themselves and their guests. Regular competitions are arranged during the year and the calendar culminates with the annual National Championships. Teams have victoriously represented Bermuda in various overseas tournaments and international players are brought in to give general clinic and training sessions. There are annual local championships and a major international tournament.

Bermuda Sub-Aqua Club
Admiralty House,
Spanish Point,
Pembroke
Tel: 293 – 9531

The group organises dives for its members at various times of the year, as well as organising training sessions, lectures and slide or movie shows. Members are also very conservation-conscious and frequently participate in group efforts to clear accumulated debris from the coastal waters. They also serve as a consulting body on matters relating to reef and wreck protection, and provide instructors to train amateurs in the skills of diving.

Bermuda Track and Field Association

The National Stadium,
Devonshire
Tel: 295 – 8574

It is under the auspices of this association that virtually every major athletic event occurs. It acts as a governing body for conventional track and field meets, and also supervises the staging of many road-racing attractions. In addition to arranging the Bermudian National Championships, it helps to organise group and individual training sessions through a programme directed by the National Athletic Coach. Competitions are arranged on a regular basis and athletes of all ages are encouraged to participate in international meets, including the Commonwealth Games and the Olympics. In 1988, Clarence 'Nicky' Saunders became the Commonwealth record holder for the high jump.

Among the major annual events which occur under the auspices of the BTFA, and which attract athletes from all over the world are: The International Marathon and the International 10km Race — both held in late January. There is also the highly regarded Annual International Triathlon, the brainchild of businessman Pat O'Riordan. Participation in each of these has now become a featured part of individual training programmes for many of the world's leading athletes.

Bermuda Water-Ski Centre

Robinson's Marina,
Somerset
Tel: 234 – 3354

Although this is a business venture, it is worth inclusion here in that it is the focal point for all those who are serious about the sport. The guiding light for the group is Kent Richardson, the most prominent water-skier Bermuda has ever produced and the first ever to secure a world ranking at the international competitions.

Yachting and Sailing

Boating is as natural to Bermudians as Alpine-skiing is to the Austrians. Events have been organised in various parts of these islands since they were first settled. Today, Bermuda is a magnet for a host of local and international sailing events, ranging from trans-Atlantic races, to the celebrated Newport-Bermuda Race and numerous in-shore and offshore competitions. Bermudian sailors have joined the crews of 'Tall Ships' races and have successfully taken part in many Olympics. In October 1985, Bermudian sailor Penny Simmons became the World Champion in the IOD racing class. This also happens to be the only country in the world where regular races are held for Bermuda fitted dinghies. There are several sailing clubs in Bermuda, each with its own calendar of events for various types of boats and races.

The islands' sailing clubs are:

East End Mini Yacht Club, Convict Bay, St George   Tel: 297 – 8202

Royal Bermuda Yacht Club, Albuoy's Point, Hamilton
Tel: 295 – 2214

Royal Hamilton Amateur Dinghy Club, 'Mangroville', Paget
Tel: 236 – 5432

Spanish Point Boat Club, Spanish Point, Pembroke
Tel: 293 – 9511

St George Dinghy and Sports Club, St George   Tel: 297 – 1612

A variety of other sports have grown considerably in popularity during the last few decades and have continued to attract substantial followings among Bermudians. Among this diverse range of interest which now enjoy organised and regular activities are: field hockey, power-boat racing, motor-cross/scrambling, windsurfing, table-tennis, netball, bowling, volleyball and go-kart racing. In each of these, Bermuda has managed to provide individuals or teams adequately skilled and equipped to represent either the country or their clubs at overseas venues. In the 1976 Montreal Olympics Bermudian boxing gained the spotlight when Clarence Hill won the bronze medal; Quinn Paynter boxed successfully in the Seoul Olympics.

Some of the less-established sports do not have a formal office nor the luxury of a regular home-base, operating instead from the home of one of the members. For this reason, specific and permanent addresses are not always available for each sport and contact telephone numbers may alter. Questions relating to sporting activities in Bermuda may always be directed to specific associations, or to:

The Director,
The Department of Youth and Sport,
Old Fire Station Building,
81 Court Street,
Hamilton HM 12   Tel: 295 – 0855

| Appendices |

A Bermuda Government Ministries

The following are official Ministries of the Bermuda Government. They may be contacted for general information and assistance. Each will also be able to suggest alternative departments or agencies for specific requirements.

Ministry for Community and Cultural Affairs
Old Fire Station Building, 81 Court Street, Hamilton HM12
Tel: 292 – 1681

Ministry for Education
Old Hospital Building, 7 Point Finger Road, Paget DV 04
Tel: 236 – 6904

Ministry for the Environment
Government Administration Building, 30 Parliament Street,
Hamilton HM 12 Tel: 295 – 5151

Ministry of Finance
Government Administration Building, 30 Parliament Street,
Hamilton HM 12 Tel: 295 – 5151

Ministry for Health and Social Services
Old Hospital Building, 7 Point Finger Road, Paget DV 04
Tel: 236 – 0224

Ministry for Tourism
Global House, 43 Church Street, Hamilton HM 12 Tel: 292 – 0023

Ministry for Transport
Global House, 43 Church Street, Hamilton HM 12 Tel: 292 – 2463

Ministry for Works and Housing
Post Office Building, 56 Church Street, Hamilton HM 12
Tel: 295 – 5151

Ministry for Youth, Sport and Recreation
Old Fire Station Building, 81 Court Street, Hamilton HM 12
Tel: 295 – 0855

N.B. It should be noted that the titles of Government Ministries may be changed or altered at the discretion of the Premier in power at any particular time.

B Galleries

The following list is not intended to be a complete directory of all galleries in Bermuda. Rather it represents those businesses which have established a reputation for dealing mainly or partly in Bermudian artwork. Prints and originals are regularly available from them and most arrange group or solo exhibitions of local artists.

The Windjammer Gallery
Cnr. Reid and King Streets,
Hamilton

Carries a variety of Bermudian and imported artwork — originals and prints. Among the Bermudian artists represented are painters Susan Curtis, Molly Critchley and Bruce Stuart and photographer Graeme Outerbridge. Also regularly featured are local scenes by Canadian Sue Quarles and American watercolourists Helen Bertles and Cecile Johnston.

Heritage House
Front Street,
Hamilton

This gallery houses a great range of artwork, from original paintings by Bermudian and European artists through to imported figurines and antiques. Invariably in stock are prints and original watercolours by most local artists. The gallery also carries a selection of marine paintings, including those by Deryck Foster and Bermudian Stephen Card.

Pegasus
Pitts Bay Road,
Hamilton

Located opposite the Hamilton Princess Hotel, this gallery houses an extensive supply of Bermudian maps, prints and cards. Additionally, there is always a fascinating display of hundreds of genuine old engravings and prints from all over the world.

Bridge House Art Gallery
off King's Square,
St George

Specialises solely in Bermudian arts and crafts, and has an extensive stock of prints. In particular, original paintings are always available by local artists Joanne Linberg Birdsey, Pamela Darrell, Otto Trott, Paul Smith, Jill Amos Raine and Ruth Masters Fountain. Always on view is a range of work by batikist Amy Evans, plus an exhibit of the unique craft of Bermuda's leading dollmaker, Kath Bell. Bermuda's unique architecture can be seen in a full range of ceramic cottages, the work of Bob and Dee Massey.

Dockyard Arts Centre
The Dockyard,
Somerset

Situated in one of the buildings directly facing the entrance to the Maritime Museum, this business houses an exhibition area and also separate rooms in which various artists work. Among those who often exhibit here are Bermudians Charles Zuill (painter); Elmer Midgett (cut-glass artist); paintings by Sharon Wilson and Judith Gardener, and posters by graphic designer Michael Swan are on view. A good selection of local prints is available.

The Gallery
The Emporium Building,
Front Street,
Hamilton

This shop has a varied selection of interesting paintings, prints, jewellery and crafts made by Bermudian and overseas artists. It is adjacent to the statue 'Gina' by Desmond Fountain and is appropriately housed in the building designed by Sjur Linberg, husband of artist Joanne Birdsey.

The Art Gallery
The City Hall
Hamilton

This gallery is owned by the City of Hamilton and is used by the Bermuda Society of Arts for a considerable variety of exhibitions which they hold throughout the year. General membership shows are arranged so as to rotate with various individual and group exhibitions. The gallery also hosts the annual primary and secondary school students' art displays, during the spring term.

Carole Holding Studio
Featherbed Alley,
St George

This small business sells primarily the prints and original watercolours of this particular artist.

The Portcullis
opposite Dowling's Marina,
St George

Although not a conventional gallery, this property is well worth visiting for its varied display of East End artwork. Owner Tony Block is also Bermuda's leading expert on the making of chess sets and heraldic shields.

Other major businesses which have established specific departments carrying a wide range of local arts and crafts include:

A.S. Coopers, Front Street, Hamilton

Triminghams, Front Street, Hamilton

Pearman Watlington, Front Street, Hamilton

The Bermuda Galleries, Washington Lane, Hamilton

C Churches

Bermuda is very well-endowed with churches and most of the major donominations are represented.

The list below is intended to reflect this diversity. It is not a complete listing of every church in Bermuda. Interested persons should contact any affiliates for specific or additional information.

African Methodist Episcopal

Allen Temple	Tel: 234 – 0433
Bethel, Shelly Bay	Tel: 293 – 0605
Bright Temple	Tel: 236 – 0364
Heard Chapel	Tel: 292 – 3949
Mt Zion	Tel: 238 – 2379
Richard Allen	Tel: 297 – 0239
St Luke, St David's Island	Tel: 297 – 1564
St Paul	Tel: 292 – 0505
St Philip, Harrington Sound Rd, Smiths	Tel: 293 – 0882
Vernon Temple	Tel: 238 – 0515

Anglican Church

Holy Trinity Cathedral, Hamilton	Tel: 292 – 4033
Christ Church, Devonshire	Tel: 236 – 3671
St Paul's, Paget	Tel: 236 – 5880
St John's, Pembroke	Tel: 292 – 0299
St Peter's, St George	Tel: 297 – 0216
St Monica's, Pembroke	Tel: 292 – 3337
St Mark's, Smiths	Tel: 236 – 8360
St James', Somerset	Tel: 234 – 2025
St Anne's, Southampton	Tel: 238 – 0370
Christ Church, Warwick	Tel: 236 – 5744

Apostolic Faith Church

Rehoboth Church of God, Warwick	Tel: 236 – 8607

Baptist

Emmanuel Baptist Church, Hamilton	Tel: 295 – 6555
First Baptist Church, Devonshire	Tel: 236 – 7212
First Baptist Church, Southampton	Tel: 238 – 0036
Wellington Baptist Church, St George	Tel: 297 – 0666

Bethel Church of God in Christ Mission

North Street, Hamilton	Tel: 295 – 2348

Brethren

Cobbs Hill Gospel Church, Warwick	Tel: 236 – 9413
Crawl Gospel Hall, Hamilton Parish	Tel: 293 – 0593
Paget Gospel Chapel, Paget	Tel: 236 – 2254
St George's Gospel Hall, St George	Tel: 297 – 1635
Calvary Gospel Chapel, Southampton	Tel: 234 – 3250
White Hill Gospel Hall, Sandys	Tel: 234 – 0496

Christian Scientist

First Church of Christ, Hamilton	Tel: 292 – 6030

Church of Christ

Church of Christ, Devonshire	Tel: 236 – 2745
Church of Christ, Somerset	Tel: 234 – 2972

Church of God

Angle Street, Hamilton	Tel: 292 – 2300
North Shore, Pembroke	Tel: 295 – 6080
Sound View Rd, Sandys	Tel: 234 – 0973

Church of God of Prophecy

Curving Avenue, Hamilton	Tel: 292 – 4074

Church of Christ of Latter Day Saints

5 Ferrars Lane, Hamilton	292 – 7068

Church of the Nazarene

Collector's Hill, South Shore, Smiths	Tel: 236 – 0227

Ethiopian Orthodox Church

Old Military Road, St George   Tel: 297 – 8411

Evangelical

Evangelical Church, Paget   Tel: 236 – 2294

Jehovah's Witnesses

St George's Congregation	Tel: 297 – 1163
Hamilton Congregation	Tel: 295 – 4507
Heron Bay Congregation, Southampton	Tel: 234 – 0389
Somerset Congregation	Tel: 238 – 1706

Jewish

Jewish Community of Bermuda   Tel: 236 – 3151

Lutheran

Peace Lutheran Church, Paget   Tel: 235 – 5330

Methodist

Wesley Methodist Church, Hamilton	Tel: 292 – 0418
Cobbs Hill Methodist Church, Warwick	Tel: 236 – 8586
Grace Methodist Church, Pembroke	Tel: 292 – 1821
Ebenezer Church, St George	Tel: 297 – 1771
Marsden Memorial Methodist Church, Smiths	Tel: 293 – 8422
Port Royal Circuit, Southampton	Tel: 238 – 1945

Muslims

Masjid Muhammad No.1, Hamilton   Tel: 292 – 5986

New Testament Church of God (Pentecostal)

Dundonald Street, Hamilton	Tel: 292 – 5214
Cedar Hill, Warwick	Tel: 236 – 5722
Jubilee Road, Devonshire	Tel: 292 – 5214
Smith's Hill, Pembroke	Tel: 295 – 1762
Somerset Road, Sandys	Tel: 234 – 2427

Pentecostal Assemblies of Canada

Evening Light, Pembroke	Tel: 292 – 4869
Paget Christian Assembly, Paget	Tel: 295 – 0325
West Pembroke Assembly, Pembroke W.	Tel: 292 – 2932

Presbyterian Church of Scotland

Christ Church, Warwick	Tel: 236 – 4835

St Andrew's Presbyterian Church

St Andrew's Church, Hamilton	Tel: 292 – 5891

Roman Catholic Church

St Theresa's Cathedral, Hamilton	Tel: 292 – 0607
St Anthony's, Warwick	Tel: 238 – 1784
St Josephs, Somerset	Tel: 234 – 2321
St Michael's, Paget	Tel: 236 – 2166
St Patrick's, Smiths	Tel: 236 – 9866
Stella Maris, St George	Tel: 297 – 1512

Salvation Army

Divisional Headquarters, Hamilton	Tel: 292 – 0601
Cedar Hill Citadel, Warwick	Tel: 236 – 6936
Hamilton Citadel	Tel: 292 – 3195
Shelly Bay Corps	Tel: 293 – 0236
Somerset Corps	Tel: 234 – 0427
St David's Outpost	Tel: 297 – 0450
St George's Corps	Tel: 297 – 0807
White Hill Corps, Southampton	Tel: 234 – 0623

Seventh Day Adventists

Roberts Avenue, Devonshire	Tel: 292 – 6927
King Street, Hamilton	Tel: 292 – 4276
Crawl Hill, Hamilton Parish	Tel: 293 – 0557
Middle Road, Southampton	Tel: 238 – 1080
St George's	Tel: 297 – 1434
Beacon Hill Rd, Somerset	Tel: 234 – 2979
South Shore, Warwick	Tel: 236 – 2813
West Pembroke Church, Pembroke	Tel: 292 – 5696

Twentieth Century Gospel Crusades of America Inc.

Pentecostal Faith Revival Temple, Hamilton   Tel: 292 – 4090

United Holy Churches of America (Pentecostal)

Warwick Holiness Church	Tel: 236 – 2723
Beulah Tabernacle, Somerset	Tel: 234 – 0633
Faith Tabernacle, Watford Island	Tel: 234 – 0305
Gospel Tabernacle, Hamilton Parish	Tel: 293 – 1283
House of Prayer, Pembroke	Tel: 292 – 1780
St George's Holy Church, Somers Playhouse	Tel: 297 – 0159

Worldwide Church of God

Melbourne House, Hamilton   Tel: 292 – 6266

MACMILLAN CARIBBEAN GUIDES SERIES
Titles available

Antigua and Barbuda: The Heart of the Caribbean – Dyde
The Bahamas: A Family of Islands – Saunders
Barbados: The Visitor's Guide – Hoyos
The Islands of Bermuda: Another World – Raine
Belize: Ecotourism in Action – Cutlack
Cuba: Official Guide – Gravette
Curaçao Close-Up – Heiligers-Halabi
Dominica: Isle of Adventure – Honychurch
Grenada: Isle of Spice – Sinclair
Jamaica: Fairest Isle: An Introduction and Guide – Sherlock
  and Preston
Montserrat: Emerald Isle of the Caribbean – Fergus
Nevis: Queen of the Caribees – Gordon
St Kitts: Cradle of the Caribbean – Dyde
St Lucia: Helen of the West Indies – Ellis
St Vincent and the Grenadines – Sutty
Trinidad and Tobago: A Guide and Introduction – Taylor
The Turks and Caicos Islands: Lands of Discovery – Smithers